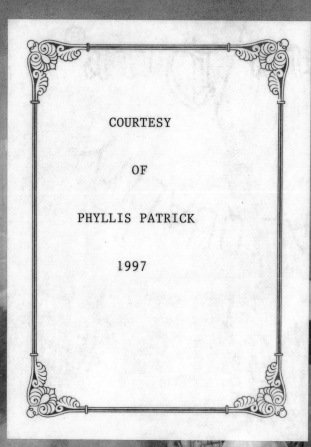

CONTENTS

◆

Introduction

Today we take quick, easy transportation for granted. We can jump into the car and be in the next town in less than an hour. It is possible to catch a plane and be halfway around the world in half a day. Human beings have even traveled outside the Earth's atmosphere, as far as the Moon.

But transportation has not always been so easy. Even at the beginning of this century, travel for most people meant a tramp across the fields from one end of a farm to the other or a weekly walk to the nearest market town. Few people left their native area.

Gradually, over thousands of years, a number of innovations made traavel more straightforward. The process began in the ancient world, probably around 6,000 years ago in the Middle East, with the invention of the wheel. This was a huge step forward, but wheeled vehicles were even more effective when the engineers

of the Persian and Roman Empires built the first good roads.

Meanwhile, the shipwrights of the great Egyptian civilization had made their own contribution to travel, building the first sailing ships and inventing the rudder with which to steer them.

Another group of developments came with the Industrial Revolution that swept across Britain and then Europe and America in the eighteenth and nineteenth centuries. The development of the steam engine led to the start of the railroad. As the iron rails snaked their way across Europe and the United States, transportation became quicker and more straightforward, affecting everything from trade to warfare. Steam engines were also used to power ships, making it easier for people to travel

long distances – and even from Europe to Australia or America to start a new life.

A host of new ideas have transformed transportation in the last 100 years or so. Many were linked to the invention of the internal combustion engine – the powerful, lightweight unit that made both cars and aircraft possible. Still faster vehicles, capable of taking people through the air and even into space, have appeared with the advent of jet engines and rockets.

This book tells the fascinating stories of all these ideas, illustrating the main developments in the history of transportation from the wheel to the space rocket. It shows how the world, which seemed vast and mysterious to our ancestors, seems to have shrunk, because it is so easy to travel around today.

PHILIP WILKINSON

THE WHEEL

About 5,000 years ago, an unknown inventor brought about a transport revolution by making the first wheeled cart.

L iving without the wheel was not as difficult as we might imagine today. For one thing, the tracks and pathways of ancient times were so narrow and uneven that wheeled vehicles would not have been much use. It was better to rely on sure-footed beasts of burden such as mules, llamas, camels, and horses. Loads were balanced on the animal's back or carried in baskets slung on each side. Slavery was common in ancient civilizations, so humans were also used as beasts of burden.

ROLLING ALONG

Heavy loads were often pulled or pushed. Sometimes the load was put on rollers made from tree trunks. This was a good way to move large building stones over short distances, but as there were no proper roads, it was not very good for longer journeys.

The sled or sleigh was another early means of transport. It was fairly easy to make, and its runners could glide over most surfaces if they were not too rocky.

△ *A travois was one of the best methods of pulling heavy loads before the invention of the wheeled cart.*

THE FIRST WHEELS

The first wheels were usually made of wood. In areas with lots of timber, they were sometimes made of one solid piece of wood (1), but most were made from three pieces of wood joined together (2).

In places where there was no wood available, wheels made from stone were used (3). To make wooden wheels lighter, people began to cut holes in the solid wood (4). Some wheels were made with a strong crossbar and struts to add strength (5). Eventually, the spoked wheel (6) was invented, combining lightness with strength.

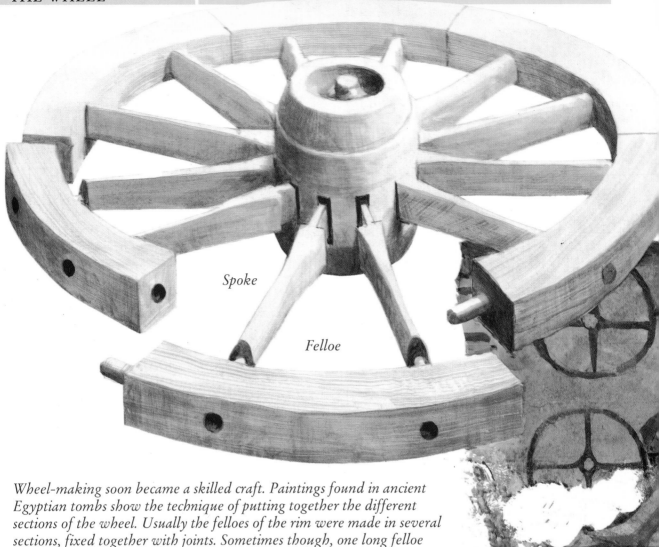

Spoke

Felloe

Wheel-making soon became a skilled craft. Paintings found in ancient Egyptian tombs show the technique of putting together the different sections of the wheel. Usually the felloes of the rim were made in several sections, fixed together with joints. Sometimes though, one long felloe was made by heating and bending a strip of wood.

Sleds were in use in Europe by 5000 B.C. and had probably also been invented independently in other parts of the world by then. They are still used for transport in polar regions.

Another type of vehicle, the "travois," was even more adaptable. It was made of two wooden poles arranged in a V-shape with the point towards the animal pulling it. The open ends trailed on the ground behind. A light framework or net filled the space between the poles to support the load. For traveling people such as the nomads of Central Asia and the North American Indians, the travois had the advantage that the poles could be separated overnight and used as tent supports.

THE FIRST WHEELS

No one knows exactly when or where the wheel was invented, but it was probably about 6,000 years ago in the Middle East. A clay tablet from Erech, Mesopotamia, dated about 3500 B.C., has a picture of a sleigh mounted on four solid wheels. This was about the same time as a wheel was first used for making pottery.

By 2500 B.C., wooden-wheeled carts seem to have been widely used in the ancient civilizations of the Middle East and in the Indus Valley in India. When the British archaeologist Sir Leonard Woolley (1880–1960) excavated the city of Ur in the 1920s, he found the remains of several wheeled vehicles. Similar remains have also been found in other Middle Eastern and Indian locations. By the first century A.D., the use of wheels had spread through the Mediterranean, northwards through Europe to Scandinavia and eastwards to China.

ACROSS THE ATLANTIC

Although the ancient civilizations of North, Central and South America were

advanced in many ways, they never discovered the wheel. When Europeans began to settle in the Americas in the sixteenth century, they took knowledge of the wheel with them. Three centuries later, it was the wheels of carts and wagon trains that enabled the far west of North America to be settled by pioneers.

As knowledge of the wheel spread throughout the ancient world, there were many improvements. It is possible that the first wheels were made of single discs of wood or even stone, but the earliest carts found by archaeologists had wheels made from three pieces. Three shaped pieces of wood were joined together by two or more crosspieces at right angles.

WHEEL AND AXLE

There were two ways of connecting the wheel to its axle. In some vehicles, the axle was fixed to the vehicle and the wheel turned around the end of it. This method worked well for light vehicles. In heavier vehicles, the wheel was fixed to the axle and the whole axle turned as the vehicle moved.

Fixed axle

Rotating axle

This type of wheel probably developed after the discovery that metal could be worked and fashioned into tools and nails. A metal saw would have been needed to cut wood accurately enough to make the three main pieces of the wheel, and copper nails were often driven round the finished edge to protect it from wear and tear.

WHEELS AT WAR

All through history, new inventions have often been quickly adopted for use in war, and the needs of warfare have often led to improvements. The story of the wheel follows this pattern.

Wheeled vehicles enabled large numbers of troops to be carried quickly into battle, surprising the enemy with a moving target that was difficult to hit.

Pictures of two-wheeled war chariots are shown on items found in the royal tombs of the city of Ur, dating from about 3000 B.C. At first, they were probably used to carry kings into battle, but they were soon adapted as troop-carriers.

LIGHTENING THE LOAD

It was probably the use of war chariots that led to the next important step forward in wheeled transport. This was the spoked wheel. Chariots needed to be fast and maneuverable. Solid wheels made them heavy, cumbersome and difficult to turn. The first stage in the development of the spoked wheel was to remove some of the solid wood between the wheel's outer rim and its hub. This made the wheel lighter, but could also weaken it.

By about 1400 B.C. in Egypt, and about

CHARIOT RACES

The ancient Greeks developed chariot racing as a sport. It was a grueling test of the riders' courage. The two-wheeled chariots were specially designed for racing. They were lightly built and carried only one person. Unlike the drivers of war chariots, the racing driver was seated. A rail at each side protected him from the wheels and enabled him to take sharp bends in safety.

Chariot races were an important part of the ancient Olympic Games. Competitors had to drive their chariots around a course which had a post at each end. The greatest skill was needed to make each turn in safety as close to the post as possible. As the competitors maneuvered their positions for the tight turns, the spectators cheered and yelled with excitement.

*An early
Scandinavian
cart*

100 years later in China, tools and woodworking skills had reached a stage where wheels could be made in separate sections of hub, spokes and rim, and then joined together. The rim was sometimes made in several pieces, called "felloes," held together with joints.

Another method was to heat and bend a long strip of wood into a circular rim, fixing the spokes into it afterwards to hold its shape. The wheelwright's craft became a specialized and highly skilled branch of carpentry, demanding the precise use of tools and a good eye for the quality of wood. The ancient Greeks used two different types of spoked wheel. For carts, they made heavier

wheels with crossbars across the rim and strengthening pieces of wood in the middle to form the hub. Chariots had wheels with four, six or eight spokes set into the inside edge of the rim.

NORTHERN SKILLS

The Celtic peoples of northern Europe added their skills to the development of wheeled transport. Experts in working metal, they also had the advantage of plentiful supplies of wood. The Celts made iron tools for wheelwrights to use, and also developed a method of "shoeing" their wheels with iron tires. The tires were usually placed red-hot over the rim and then plunged into water,

It was not until the seventeenth century that vehicles began to be fitted with springs. Before that passengers and goods had no protection at all from the jolting caused by bumpy roads.

so that the iron contracted tightly over the rim. As the metal shrank, it hardened, giving the wheel added strength. The Celts often used different woods for the different parts of their wheels. The spokes might be made of hornbeam, the rim of a single piece of ash and the hub of oak.

WEAR AND TEAR

Many historians think that the Celts may also have come up with the first solution to another problem. Whether the wheels were fixed to an axle and went round with it, or rotated individually on their own hubs, the continuous movement caused wear. In time, either the axle or the wheels would become loose and would have to be replaced. Some Celtic carts have been found to have grooves

in the hubs. These grooves could have held wooden rods which turned between the hub and the axle, making a simple bearing. It would have been far easier and cheaper to replace the rods than to fit new wheels or axles.

The design of the spoked wheel bound with an iron tire changed little between ancient Celtic times and the coming of the railways. It was suitable for all kinds of vehicles, from royal carriages to humble farm carts, and is still in use today. The major change was the introduction of springs in the seventeenth century. At first, these were leather straps attached to the axles of passenger carriages to take the weight of the vehicle's body and give a smoother ride. Later, steel springs of various shapes were fitted between the axles and the vehicle body.

Ball bearings between the wheel hub and the axle were also introduced in the eighteenth century. They not only reduced wear on the hub and axle, but also needed less maintenance. Previously, wheel hubs had to be thoroughly greased before each journey, but ball bearings contained a supply of oil which could last for weeks or even months.

REINVENTING THE WHEEL

It was only when the heavier loads and faster speeds of the railways and later of motorized road vehicles demanded stronger wheels that engineers began to rethink the design of the wheel. The railways gradually abandoned spoked wheels for solid metal. On the roads, wheel design had to change when the inflatable rubber tire was invented.

The first rubber tires were made of solid rubber, and these continued in use, especially for heavy goods wagons, until the 1920s. The air-filled leather tire first appeared in 1845. It was the invention of a Scotsman, Robert Thomson (1822–73). Four of his tires were fitted to a horse-drawn carriage and driven

for nearly 1,000 miles (1,600 kilometers) before they wore out. But the public was not impressed, and Thomson's invention was soon forgotten.

Forty-two years later, another Scot, John Boyd Dunlop (1840–1921), made the first air-filled or "pneumatic" tire, using a tube inside a rubber outer casing. His invention was taken up enthusiastically by racing cyclists, and so the first pneumatic tires were designed for bicycles.

A few years later, cars began to appear on the roads, and they too adopted pneumatic tires. The first car wheels had wire spokes like bicycles, but by the 1930s, these were being replaced by pressed steel plates. The evolution of the modern wheel was complete.

▽ *The first tires were made from solid rubber, but pneumatic tires filled with air proved more successful.*

ROADS

*Fine roads were built by the Persians,
the Chinese and the Romans. Later in history,
a journey by road became a nightmare
for travelers who had to face rocks, potholes,
mud and floods.*

T he first people on earth lived by hunting and gathering food, roaming from one place to another in search of food and shelter. They had not yet begun to cultivate the land, to keep animals or to live together in communities. Their movements were haphazard, and they tended to avoid places where other people might have been before them searching for food. There was no need for roads or even for tracks to take the people from one place to another.

TRADE AND TRAVEL

All this changed once people settled down, grew crops and raised livestock. They began to trade, exchanging their surplus farm produce for other goods. Some people specialized in crafts such as making pots, carpentry or metalwork, and they often set up their businesses in

△ *The Persian Royal Road, built c. 3500 B.C., was used by the army to move quickly around the empire to put down uprisings and rebellions.*

▷ *The Romans built a network of roads around their empire. The roads were so strong and thick, they were more like underground walls.*

villages or towns. These developments created the need to travel, and the need for tracks between settlements.

These early tracks were paths worn across the landscape by traders and their pack animals. They developed into recognized routes because they avoided obstacles such as mountains or difficult river crossings. Travelers usually chose open country where they were less likely to be attacked by wild animals or hostile tribes, so many tracks ran along ridges or across open desert.

Milestones were placed along Roman roads so that the army could tell how far it had traveled.

MILITARY ROADS

The ancient civilizations of the Middle East were the first to turn these rough tracks into roads. There were roads connecting Babylonia and Egypt, and linking such cities as Assur and Babylon. Parts of these roads, dating from about 700 B.C., have survived. In some ways, they were surprisingly modern in the way they were made. A foundation of rubble and gravel was covered with a layer of bricks, and the road surface was made of stone slabs. They were built to last.

As the great empires of the ancient world expanded, their rulers built roads so that they could communicate more easily with their distant corners. Although they were often used by traders, roads were built mainly for use by soldiers. The Persian Royal Road, built round about 3500 B.C. and in use until about 300 B.C., was one of these. It was a network of roads which ran from Susa on the Persian Gulf to places such as

Jerusalem, Nineveh and the Black Sea. The empires of China, Egypt, ancient Greece and the Incas of South America also had their road networks, built by slaves.

ROMAN ROAD-BUILDERS

The Romans brought road-building to a fine art. Their network spread out from Rome across their empire, north to south through Italy, France and Spain, and eastwards to Turkey. After the Romans invaded Britain in 54 B.C., they created roads which until recently formed the country's major road network.

The roads of the Roman empire covered about 53,000 miles (85,000 kilometers). They were built mainly to link the army garrisons which controlled the provinces. If trouble broke out, more troops could quickly be brought to take charge. To help troop commanders check that they had met their targets of miles marched per day, the Romans placed milestones by the side of their roads.

The Romans were expert engineers and surveyors. This enabled them to build their roads straight except where it was necessary to avoid an obstruction. The high point of their road-building was the Appian Way, the great military road leading to Rome. In some places, the foundations were 5 feet (1.5 meters) deep.

Building began by digging a deep trench. A layer of sand or mortar was placed at the bottom, and large flat stones were laid on top. Then came a layer of smaller stones mixed with lime, a layer of gravel and coarse sand mixed with lime, and finally a top surface of volcanic lava.

Like all Roman roads, the Appian Way was curved or "cambered" so that rainwater would flow away.

THE DISAPPEARING ROADS

By A.D. 400, the Roman empire was divided and on its way into history. The roads that the Romans had left behind in Europe gradually deteriorated for lack of maintenance, and in many places they disappeared altogether.

The people of the Middle Ages had little use for roads. They relied mainly on horses and pack animals, which could use the older hilltop tracks, rather than on wheeled vehicles. But as towns and cities grew in size from about 1500 onwards, the need for communication and trade increased. At this time, a journey of any length at all in a wheeled vehicle must have been a nightmare. Cartwheels made deep ruts in winter, and the hooves of the

THE ROAD TO EMPIRE

Most road-building in the ancient world was for military use. As empires expanded, rulers needed to ensure that their armies could move about with ease.

The roads built by the ancient Chinese were designed for use by marching soldiers. In mountainous areas, they included flights of stone steps.

The Romans' roads, too, were for use by the army. They were planned to allow columns of soldiers to march side by side in fours without breaking ranks.

Military road-building continued until recent times. In the eighteenth century, the English army built roads in Scotland to control rebellious Scottish clans.

After the fall of the Roman Empire, the surface of many Roman roads deteriorated gradually. The roads were not used so much because they were now used by pack animals rather than soldiers.

animals pulling them ground the tracks into seas of mud. Potholes appeared where stones had been washed away by storms. It is not surprising that a journey of more than a few miles was thought of as a dangerous adventure, and few people traveled at all except in the summer months.

PAY AS YOU GO

Communities were encouraged to maintain good roads in their own areas, but not all of them did so. In any case, this did not solve the problem of the gaps between one area and another. The answer found in Britain and some other European countries was to build toll or turnpike roads along major routes. Travelers paid a small fee at tollhouses positioned every few miles. The fees were intended to be used to maintain the roads, but they often went into the

and this sparked off a new interest in methods of road-building. It would have been too costly to copy Roman methods, but in 1764, a Frenchman, Pierre Tresaguet (1716–96), came up with a plan based on Roman ideas but much easier and cheaper to build. His roads were no more than eleven inches (twenty-five centimeters) thick. The base was a closely-packed layer of large, flat stones. This was covered with a layer of much smaller, broken stones to give a smooth surface. To ensure that surface water drained off the roads, they were given a cambered top so that the middle was about six inches (fifteen centimeters) higher than the sides.

NEW ROADS FOR EUROPE

Tresaguet's first road was built from Paris to Toulouse, and onwards to the border with Spain. It was so successful that his road-building system was adopted in many

John McAdam and Thomas Telford pioneered new road-building methods in the eighteenth century.

pockets of the collectors. Even if this did not happen, the people responsible for keeping the roads in good repair often had no idea how to do their job.

The bad state of the roads became a serious problem for traders and travelers,

countries of Europe. It was copied in Britain by John Metcalf (1717–1810), who built 200 miles (300 kilometers) of roads in the north of England. He improved on Tresaguet's ideas by adding a ditch on each side of roads to give extra drainage.

ROAD SURFACES

A good road must be built on a solid base to provide support for the weight of passing vehicles.

McAdam's roads had a cambered foundation with two four-inch (ten-centimeter) courses of stones covered by a top layer of fine stones, and a drainage channel at each side.

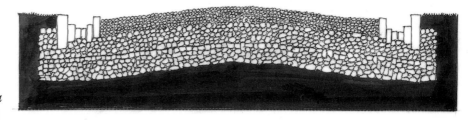

Tresaguet's roads were supported on a layer of heavy stones pushed into a stone base. Above this were two layers of smaller stones. Retaining stones at the sides kept everything in place.

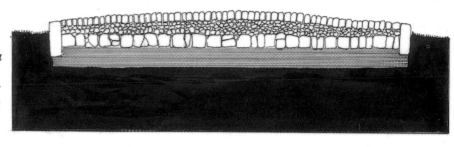

Many modern roads have a bottom layer of small stones followed by a layer of concrete, topped with a layer of tar or asphalt and another layer of asphalt above. Some have a hard shoulder with a shallow concrete foundation not designed for hard wear.

Two other British engineers made advances in the science of road-building in the early nineteenth century. They were Thomas Telford (1757–1834) and John McAdam (1756–1836). Both had the idea that the wheels of passing traffic could help to make a smooth surface for a new road by pounding the top layer into fine dust. This dust worked its way downward to the lower layers and helped to bind them together. Telford's roads had a top layer of small stones thinly covered with gravel. McAdam's roads also had a layer of small stones on the surface, but lime was added to the stone dust to make a cement-like finish.

Roads built in this way were cheap to make and the surface was adequate for fairly slow-moving, horse-drawn transport. However, they were often damaged by rainstorms or deep frost.

But while Telford and McAdam were building their roads, a new form of transport was emerging. The railways were soon in command of most passenger and goods traffic, and interest in road-building faded. After the coming of the railways, few new roads were built for the rest of the nineteenth century.

THE ROAD REVIVAL

The invention of gasoline and diesel engines tipped the balance once more in favor of roads. Faster-moving, rubber-tired vehicles loosened the stones of the old roads and created clouds of dust. The

In the eighteenth century, turnpikes were set up to collect money from road-users to improve the road quality. Today, new roads and bridges in some countries are paid for by tolls.

answer was found to be a top layer of tar which sealed the dust in and evened out bumps. In the 1900s, roads began to take on their modern appearance.

As road traffic grew in the 1920s and 1930s, the old roads, even with their new tar surfaces, proved to be inadequate.

Some were too narrow. Others had bridges that needed to be strengthened, or bends that were too tight to be taken safely at speed. Many of the gradients were too steep for safety. New roads were needed, designed for the heavy, fast-moving traffic of the motor age.

HIGH-SPEED TRAFFIC

Most countries began large road-building programs in the 1930s. The U.S. built

federal highways covering major routes, backed up with interstate highways. Germany called its new roads *autobahnen*. France built its *routes nationales* and Italy its *autostrada*. Britain was late starting its new road network, not opening its first motorway until 1959.

These new roads all had similar features. They separated traffic moving in different directions, and each had a number of lanes. Sharp bends and steep gradients were avoided, and careful signposting prepared drivers for road junctions. Tunnels or overpasses carried the new roads under or over city streets, and shoulders and embankments were landscaped to give drivers a good view ahead. Ring roads were built around major cities so that through traffic could avoid the congested city streets. Roads have once again become of vital importance to our everyday lives.

BOATS & SHIPS

From the earliest times, people realized that water could be used as a means of transport. Thousands of years of experiment and invention perfected the sailing ship as a vessel for trade and a weapon of war.

W e have to go back into prehistory to imagine how people might have discovered that water was useful for transport. Early humans settled beside rivers and lakes where there was a water supply. The fish that could be caught from the banks were an added bonus.

FLOATING ON AIR

It was probably through observing floating logs and branches that people realized that they could use water to carry themselves and their goods. The first journeys by water may have been made by people holding on to tree trunks which had been washed downriver.

Then, someone discovered that objects containing air not only floated but could support a weight in the water. The next stage was to make floats of inflated animal skins sewn together tightly. Sealed clay pots were also used as floats. When skin or clay floats were bound together to make rafts, they could support a large platform carrying people or cargo.

△ *The earliest method of travel by water was probably to hold on to a floating log.*

△ *The first rafts were probably adapted from swimming floats, made of wood, skins or pots.*

In shallow water, a raft could be driven along and steered with a pole long enough to reach to the riverbed, but this was not possible where the water was deeper. The next development was to build a light raft with raised sides which could be pushed along with a paddle.

Early civilizations developed a wide variety of craft for transport or fishing. The dugout canoe was a tree-trunk with a hollow carved or burned into the middle. Archaeologists have found remains of dugouts dating from about 6300 B.C.

△ *The coracle or quffa was one of the first craft to have high sides like a boat rather than being flat.*

But dugouts could only be made in wooded places. In some places, a large basket-shaped frame was made from thin wood or wicker and animal skins were stretched tightly over it. These craft were built with simple tools such as flint knives and bone needles. They were so light that could be picked up and carried on the

and pointed at each end to cut down the resistance of the water.

The Egyptians were also responsible for two further developments which were to change the history of travel by water. The first was the invention of the sail. Although it was easy to travel north down the Nile with the current, returning

△ *Large ships were powered by rowing slaves who sat chained to benches.*

back if necessary. Boats of this kind were in use in Assyria before 6000 B.C. They are still in use in some places. In the British Isles, they are called "coracles," and in the Middle East, "quffas."

REED BOATS

The civilization of ancient Egypt was the first to make a real effort to develop the technology of boat-building. The Egyptians lived along the River Nile, which could be sailed for about 750 miles (1,200 kilometers), but there were no large trees in the area. The first Egyptian craft were rafts made out of the reeds that grew plentifully along the banks of the Nile. The reeds were tied in bundles and then bound tightly together. From simple rafts, the Egyptians went on to make reed boats, which were equipped with oars

home was hard work using just oars and paddles. At this time, the Egyptians grew cotton and were already skilled at weaving it into cloth. Observation of woven cotton hung out to dry must have given someone the idea of using wind power to propel boats. Sailors began to equip their boats with one large sail, made from tightly woven cotton and ropes to turn the sail into the wind. Oars could be used if the wind dropped.

THE RUDDER

The second important Egyptian innovation was the rudder. At first, this was simply a large paddle fixed at the boat's stern, with ropes to turn it. This made the steering independent of the oars and made movement in the water much more precise.

Reed boats were good for sailing up and down the river, but at sea sturdier craft were needed. The Egyptians began to build wooden boats from short planks of acacia, the only wood available. These boats were built up plank by plank, forming a hollow shell. With these boats, the Egyptians built up a large sea trade, exporting corn and cotton in return for jewels, spices, wood and metal.

FRAME-BUILT BOATS

Between 1500 and 1000 B.C., a civilization grew up whose entire fortune was founded on seafaring trade. The Phoenicians lived at the eastern end of the

HOW SAILS WORK

The first sails were simply large rectangular sheets of cloth fixed to a mast at right angles to the boat. In a following wind, that is one blowing in the direction of travel, these sails used the wind efficiently to carry the boat forward. But they did not work if the wind was blowing from any other direction.

Arab fishermen in the Red Sea and the Indian Ocean were probably the first sailors to use lateen sails. The lateen is a triangular sail fixed to the mast along one side. The corner opposite the fixed side can be moved from side to side. This enables the sailor to adjust the position of the sail according to the direction of the wind. This is called "trimming." By trimming the sails, the boat can be "tacked," or driven forward on a zigzag course, even if it is sailing into the wind.

As sailing ships developed, they used combinations of square and lateen sails so that they could take advantage of all kinds of wind conditions. Each sail was controlled individually by ropes. Most ships had the square mainsails amidships to gather the wind and give the ship speed, while lateen sails at the bow and stern were trimmed to help the rudder control the ship's direction of travel.

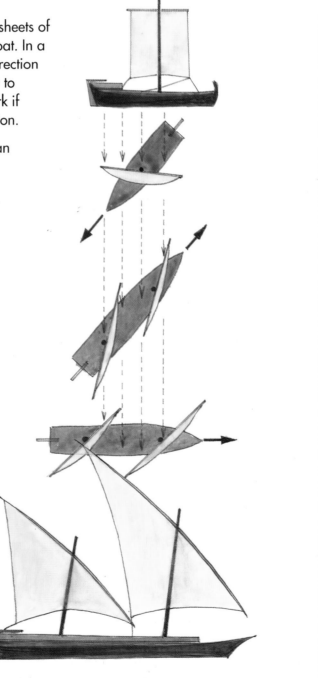

Mediterranean in what is now called Lebanon, and built the finest ships that had yet been seen. They were able to improve on Egyptian designs because they had tall cedar trees which they could use as keel and frame timbers. This meant that their ships were stronger and more suitable for long voyages at sea. For trading, they built "round ships" which traveled slowly but could carry a large amount of cargo. Their most famous craft were the Phoenician longships, the first ships to be built for battle.

Longships had large, square sails. Wind power was backed up by men with oars, sometimes in two or three banks, one above the other. Built long and narrow, longships could cut through the water at a fast pace. At their bows, they had rams to attack enemy ships. With these superior craft, the Phoenicians took command of the seas. From their home ports they explored the coasts of Africa, the Mediterranean and northwestern Europe, setting up trading stations wherever they went

CASTLES ON BOARD

Phoenician warships were designed to move in quickly to attack the enemy's fleet. If they were themselves attacked, they had little defense. The Greeks and Romans copied and improved on Phoenician ships.

The Romans gave their ships extra speed by adding a second sail at the bow, and designed a more accurate rudder with two paddles. In front of the stern, they built a structure which housed marines who were armed and ready to fight. This "castle" was to become a feature of all large sailing ships, providing protection for the crew. The front part of a ship where the crew lives is still called the "forecastle" or "fo'c'sle."

The Greeks and Romans changed the style of warfare at sea. Their warships, called "galleys," were designed to carry troops for battle on the water. The galley would attack an enemy ship, and marines would fight on the decks of both. This kind of sea warfare was to continue for hundreds of years in Europe.

LATEEN SAILS

The Romans copied the square sails of the Phoenicians, but they also used triangular or "lateen" sails. The word lateen comes from "Latin," the language of the Romans, but the triangular sail was developed many years before the days of the Roman Empire. It was first used by Arab sailors in the Red Sea and Indian Ocean. They sailed light, slim boats called "dhows," with a triangular sail which ran

SAILING SHIPS

The fastest sailing ships ever built were called "clippers." They were oceangoing ships designed to carry perishable cargoes such as fruit and grain. The first clipper, the *Ann McKim*, was built in Baltimore, Maryland, in 1832. There was keen competition for speed between clipper owners. One ship, the *Cutty Sark*, once covered 362 miles (584 kilometers) in one day's sailing. It took only sixty-nine days to sail from Australia to Britain, compared with the normal one hundred days.

The largest sailing ship ever built was the *Great Republic*, launched in the United States in 1853 and intended to sail between the USA and Australia. While being prepared for its maiden voyage, it caught fire and sank, but it was later refloated and used as a troop-carrier in the American Civil War.

△ *Egyptian shipwrights built ships from bundles of reeds or from short planks of wood joined together. The wooden boats looked like reed boats, with their high, curved ends.*

lengthways down the ship rather than across it. This enabled it to be trimmed, or turned, to take greater advantage of the wind. Roman galleys combined both kinds of sail, which made them more maneuverable in all kinds of weather.

VIKING RAIDERS

About 1,200 years ago, a new kind of ship was developed in northern Europe. The Vikings lived in Denmark, Norway and Sweden, where there was a good supply of timber. Their boats were the first to be "clinker-built," where each long plank of wood overlapped the one below.

Viking longships, powered by a large, square sail and up to eighty oarsmen, carried out raids round the coasts of Europe and as far away as Greenland and North America. There was no protection for the crew, but longships were curved upwards at the bow and stern to help prevent them taking on too much water in high seas. The bow of the ship was often decorated with a figurehead of a

carved mythical figure such as a dragon.
Viking ships were not intended for
fighting at sea. The Vikings had the best
ships and were the most fearless sailors
of their time, and were unlikely to meet
any rivals on their voyages.

THE GALLEON

After the Vikings, sail increasingly took
over from oars as the major source of
power for large ships, although oars were
still carried for when there was no wind.
By the fifteenth century, the three- or

four-masted galleon, standing high out of
the water, was being used for both trade
and war. This was the kind of ship that
took part in the great European voyages
of exploration in the sixteenth and
seventeenth centuries. In this period, too,
European nations such as Spain, Portugal,
France and Britain built up their navies
with the aim of ruling the world's oceans.
Heavy guns were introduced on ship
about 1400, and, by the eighteenth
century, a galleon could have as many
as a hundred heavy cannons aboard.

Around the world a great
variety of craft have developed
from the earliest rafts.
1 Masted outrigger canoes, South
  Pacific
2 Single masted reed boat,
  Lake Titicaca, South America
3 Modern windsurfer
4 Log raft
5 Junk, South China
6 Arabian dhow
7 Ancient Egyptian reed boat
8 Small sailing boat, South China
9 Wooden rowing boat, Europe
  and North America

By this time, there was a wide variety of ships at sea. The great battleships were backed up by smaller naval craft designed for speed and surprise attacks. Merchant ships ranged from large oceangoing galleons to small ships plying their trade along the coasts. Meanwhile, larger fishing-boats were built to range further and further from their home ports.

THE COMING OF STEAM

Towards the end of the eighteenth century, there was a development which was to signal the end of the days of sailing ships. In the 1780s, the first steamboats were built in America, driven by large oars powered by a steam engine. The boats were not a success, but other inventors took up the idea of using steam power for ships, and the next hundred years was a story of the triumph of steam and the gradual fading away of sail.

FINDING THE WAY

The first sailors had nothing to guide them except the sun by day and the stars at night. The compass was the first of a number of aids to navigation that made travel by sea safer and easier.

Sailors, aircrews, motorists and even walkers use charts or maps to help them find the way to where they want to go. There are only a very few parts of the world, on land or sea, which have not been charted or mapped today.

Thousands of years ago, however, travelers had no maps to help them. If they were sailing in sight of land or walking in an area they knew, they could rely on landmarks such as high cliffs or mountains to guide them. But on the ocean, or in the middle of a desert or forest, there are no landmarks. Travelers had to find some other means of navigation.

FOLLOWING THE SUN

Early travelers kept their eyes on the sky. They knew that the sun rose in one direction, climbed to a high point and then gradually sank until it set on the opposite side of the sky. Observing the sun's position in the sky gave them some

△ *For thousands of years, a ship in the middle of the ocean could not tell exactly where it was.*

idea of the direction they were going.

At night, travelers could use the stars. North of the equator, they looked for the North Star, directly over the North Pole, as a pointer. In the southern hemisphere, they used the group of four stars called the Southern Cross which points the way south. Navigating by the sun or the stars was, of course, possible only when the sky was clear. Many travelers must have got lost when the sky clouded over.

Traveling became much easier when it was found that a small piece of lodestone, a brownish rock made of iron oxide, would always take up the same position in a line from north to south when allowed to swing freely. Lodestone is magnetic. It reacts to the Earth's magnetic field so that the north-seeking pole of the stone is attracted to the Earth's magnetic North Pole. Someone must have observed that every time a small piece of lodestone was allowed to move

freely it took up a position in line with the sun at midday and the North Star at night. Whoever first made this discovery was the inventor of the compass.

THE CHINESE COMPASS

About 400 B.C., a Chinese writer described how overland travelers used a "south-pointer" to help them find their way. Early Chinese compasses had a spoon-shaped piece of lodestone which was free to pivot on a polished bronze plate. The handle of the spoon pointed south.

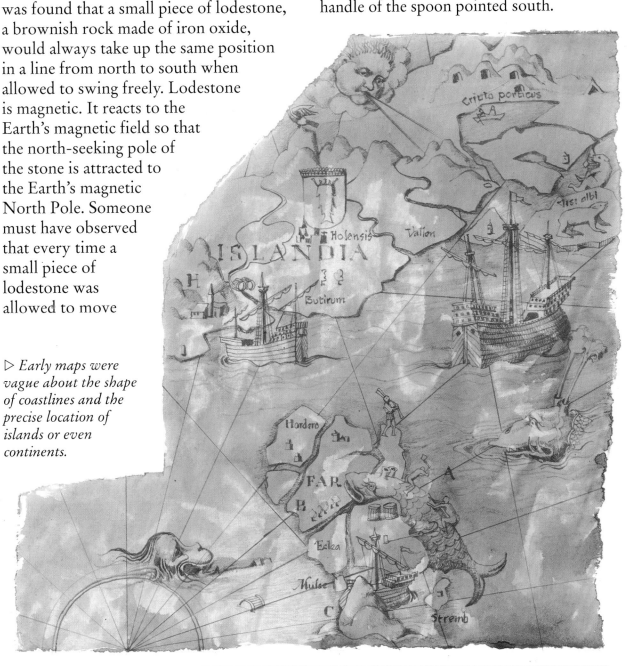

▷ *Early maps were vague about the shape of coastlines and the precise location of islands or even continents.*

The Chinese did not only use the compass for finding their way. There was an ancient Chinese belief that the exact siting of a building, including the direction it faced, was important for the happiness and good fortune of the people who lived in it. Before a house was built, an expert called a "geomancer" was called in to advise on how it should be positioned, and he used a compass to come to his decision.

WHO INVENTED THE COMPASS?

Although the first written mention of the compass was in a Chinese book, the Chinese may not have been the first people to use the instrument. Some historians believe that the ancient Egyptians, or the Olmecs of ancient Mexico, made the discovery first, perhaps as long ago as 1000 B.C. What is certain is that by early in the twelfth century AD, Chinese sailors were using the compass at sea. By this time it had been discovered that an iron needle could be magnetized by rubbing it on a piece of lodestone. The needle could then be used as a pointer by floating it on a piece of cork or wood in a bowl of water.

THE NEEDLE COMPASS

Soon after this, the compass made its first appearance in Europe. How the knowledge traveled from east to west is not certain. Perhaps it came by way of the Islamic world, through Arab sailors, but this seems unlikely since the first Islamic descriptions of the compass are slightly later than those in Europe.

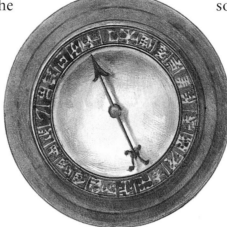

An early Chinese mariner's compass.

The first European to describe the compass was the English writer Alexander Neckham (1157–1217), in a book produced in 1187. At this time the compass needle was still being floated in water. In a book about magnetism published in 1269, the compass had taken on a more modern appearance. The needle was pivoted at the center so that it could move freely, and was placed in a box with a glass cover. This made it a far more practical instrument for use at sea.

The most important innovation was a card at the bottom of the box which showed a circle divided into 360 degrees. This meant that the use of the compass by sailors had progressed well beyond the simple purpose of finding north and south. Using the 360 degree divisions, sailors could now plot a course and make corrections when they strayed from it.

DEAD RECKONING

There was still no way that sailors could work out their exact position. The best they could do with a compass was to find out in which direction they were moving. With the help of a system called "dead reckoning," they could work out roughly how far they had traveled along their chosen course. For this, they needed a hourglass and a long piece of rope with a log tied at the end.

▷ *It took centuries for the lodestone compass (top left) to develop into the compass we recognize today (top right). Once developed, accurate sea charts could be drawn with lines to show the compass bearings to various ports.*

THE SEARCH FOR AUSTRALIA

The invention of the sextant and the chronometer in the eighteenth century provided a new spur to exploration by European sailors. One of the most famous was Captain James Cook (1728–79).

Very little was known then about Australia, New Zealand, New Guinea and the smaller islands of the southern Pacific Ocean. The position of some islands, and parts of the coast of Australia, had been roughly mapped, and many people believed they were parts of a great southern continent, "Terra Australis," that spread around the South Pole. Captain Cook's orders for his first expedition were to find out whether the southern Pacific was merely an ocean, or contained another great continent.

Cook set out in April 1769 and was away for fourteen months. On his return, he was able to report that no "great southern continent" existed. He had mapped and surveyed much of the coast of Australia, and had shown that there was open sea to the south between Australia and Antarctica.

The hourglass was big enough to mark the passing of an hour or half an hour as the sand trickled from the top half into the bottom through a narrow neck. A junior member of the ship's crew was given the job of turning the hourglass. At the same time, the rope, with knots tied at regular intervals, was paid out at the stern of the ship. A sailor counted each knot as it passed through his hands. When the top half of the hourglass was empty, the number of knots since it had been turned over enabled the navigator to work out the speed of the ship. The speed of ships at sea is still measured in "knots" today. A knot is one nautical mile (1.15 miles or 1,853 meters) per hour.

SUN AND STARS

If the sky was clear, sailors had another instrument which they could use to check their position. This was the "astrolabe," invented in Greece about 200 B.C. The astrolabe was a dial with a pointer that moved to measure the altitude of the sun or the stars in degrees. This helped sailors to calculate the time and the ship's latitude, or position north or south of the equator. There was still no way of calculating a ship's longitude, or its position east or west.

The great European voyages of discovery, such as those of Ferdinand Magellan (c. 1480–1521) and Christopher Columbus (1451–1506), were made with only the astrolabe, the compass, the hourglass and the log and line. But these were the success stories. The dead reckoning method of calculating a position was very unreliable. Variations in winds and tides, or a moment's inattention by the boy with the hourglass or the sailor with the log and line, could throw the calculations badly wrong. For every successful voyage, there were many disasters when ships ran aground or simply got lost in the vast, empty oceans.

LOCAL TIME

In 1731, an English scientist, John Hadley (1682–1744), invented the sextant. This was an instrument for measuring the altitude of the sun or stars, and was a great improvement on earlier methods such as the astrolabe. It provided an accurate measurement of the ship's latitude and of the "local time" on board ship, but it still did not help with its position east or west.

ACCURATE TIMEKEEPING

What was needed was a means of showing the time at a known position so that it could be compared with the ship's local time. The difference between the two times would show the ship's distance east or west of the line of longitude passing through the known position. British ships, and eventually all the world's shipping, took the "known position" to be Greenwich in southeast London.

The loss of ships at sea because of inaccurate navigation had become so serious by 1714 that the British Admiralty offered a prize of £20,000 to the maker of a chronometer accurate enough to keep time to within three seconds a day over a period of six weeks, even on a rough ocean voyage.

It was nearly fifty years before a clockmaker came up with the winning design. He was John Harrison (1693–1776), from Yorkshire in England. When his chronometer was tested on a voyage from London to the West Indies in 1761, it beat the Admiralty's requirements by losing only 2.7 seconds a day. For the first time, it was possible for sailors to work out their longitude as well as their latitude.

A SAFER MEANS OF TRAVEL

Although expensive at first, by about 1800, the chronometer was in general use among the western world's navies and merchant fleets.

△ *John Harrison's chronometer.*

The chronometer brought about a revolution in ocean travel. As well as directly aiding navigation, the chronometer meant that coastlines and hidden rocks could be pinpointed more accurately on maps and charts. Shipping losses fell sharply, and business people were more ready to invest in carrying goods by sea. It was from this time that great shipping and trading companies began to make fortunes for those who invested in them, and the sea became a safer place for people who worked or traveled on it.

THE STEAM ENGINE

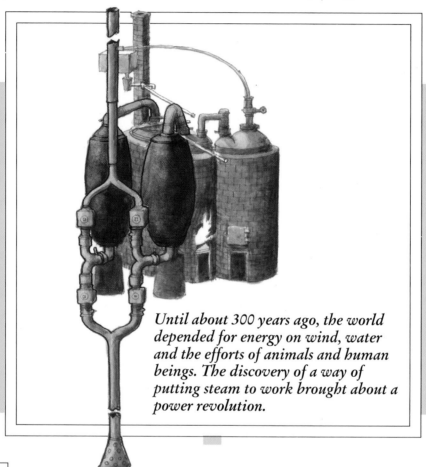

Until about 300 years ago, the world depended for energy on wind, water and the efforts of animals and human beings. The discovery of a way of putting steam to work brought about a power revolution.

T he knowledge that steam could produce energy is about 2,000 years old. An Egyptian engineer called Hero (first century B.C.) made a machine called an "aeolipile" in which steam drove round a metal sphere. The aeolipile was a toy with no practical use, but it showed that steam could be a source of energy.

The modern history of steam power began with a French scientist, Denis Papin (1647–c. 1712). He spent most of his working life experimenting with gases and vacuums. The pressure cooker was one of his inventions. Papin also designed a simple steam pump to provide the power for fountains. The pump worked, but the high pressure of water it created kept bursting the pipes. In 1690, Papin had the idea of building an engine in which steam would raise a piston inside a cylinder, creating a vacuum as it rose. This was the principle of later steam engines, but Papin never managed to make an engine that worked.

△ *Thomas Savery's steam engine, the "Miner's Friend," was made to pump water out of mines.*

THE POWER OF STEAM

For centuries, people were fascinated by the power of steam, but unable to think of a practical use for it.

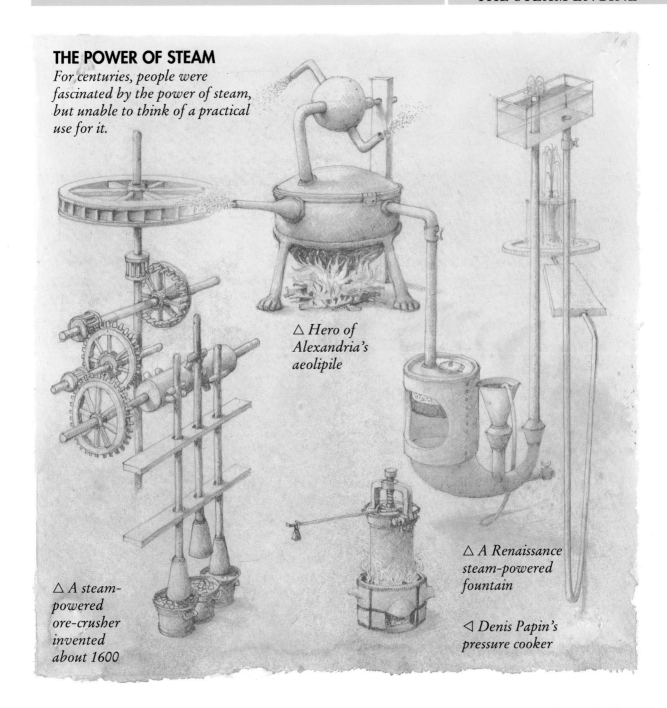

△ *Hero of Alexandria's aeolipile*

△ *A Renaissance steam-powered fountain*

◁ *Denis Papin's pressure cooker*

△ *A steam-powered ore-crusher invented about 1600*

THE MINER'S FRIEND

The first successful steam engine arose out of the urgent need to pump water out of flooded mine shafts. In 1698, an English engineer, Thomas Savery (c. 1650–1715), invented a steam pump. He called it the "Miner's Friend." It had a cylinder which was filled with steam from a boiler. When the cylinder was cooled by pouring cold water on the outside, a partial vacuum was created.

The vacuum drew water into the cylinder from the mine shaft. The Miner's Friend would pump water up only about twenty feet (six meters). If the water was any deeper, the engine became unsafe and sometimes even blew up.

Another Englishman, Thomas Newcomen (1663–1729), invented a safer steam engine that could pump from greater depths. Its cylinder was cooled by water sprayed from inside. Unlike the

OPPOSITION TO STEAM

To people who had been used to the quiet and leisurely pace of horse-drawn transport, the speed, power and noise of steam locomotives were terrifying.

The first victim of a railway accident was a British cabinet minister, Sir William Huskisson (1770–1830). At the opening of the Liverpool and Manchester Railway in 1830, he stepped into the path of the oncoming train and was killed.

Some even believed that rail travel could be dangerous. In the 1830s, an eminent Irish scientist, Dr. Dionysius Lardner (1793–1859), warned that traveling at speeds of thirty miles (forty-eight kilometers) per hour could make the brain fall apart. In Britain, Queen Victoria was persuaded to make a train journey from Windsor to London in 1842 to show that rail travel was safe.

Country people in particular were opposed to railways. They had good reason, because the noise and smoke of trains often frightened livestock grazing by the line and made horses throw their riders. Another problem was that sparks from locomotive chimneys came down in nearby fields and set fire to growing crops. But farmers later found that they benefited from railways, because trains could get their goods to market more quickly than before.

Miner's Friend, Newcomen's cylinder was open at the top. This space was filled with a piston, a circular iron plate which fitted tightly but could still slide up and down. An iron rod was fixed to the piston. As the steam from the boiling water below made the piston rise and fall, it operated a beam connected to a pump.

Like Savery's pump, Newcomen's engine used a huge amount of coal to raise steam. This did not matter when it was used in coal mines, where there was plenty of fuel. From 1712, when the first Newcomen engine was installed in a coal mine in the English Midlands, it became standard equipment in many British pits. Shafts could now be sunk deeper and more coal extracted. But where there was no coal close at hand, the cost of fuel for boiling water to raise steam was too high.

IMPROVING THE ENGINE

At this point, the best-known name in the history of steam comes into the story. James Watt (1736–1819) was a Scottish instrument maker and repairer working at the University of Glasgow. In 1763, he saw a Newcomen engine for the first time when the university sent a model in for repair. Watt was a true scientist, always questioning and experimenting. Soon he was working on ways to improve the efficiency and cut the fuel consumption of the Newcomen engine.

Watt's first improvement was to separate the heating and cooling stages of the engine's operation. Having to heat the water and then cool it in the same cylinder made the Newcomen engine slow and was also the main cause of its heavy use of fuel. Watt designed an engine with a separate condenser where the cooling process could take place. Meanwhile, the cylinder stayed hot all the time. This meant that there was no pause while the cylinder reheated.

The addition of a condenser was only one of the improvements made by James Watt. Of the others, the most important for the future of transport was his

▷ *James Watt improved on the steam engines available at the time and made steam power a practical source of power for industries.*

△ Rails were used to pull vehicles along in mines before steam trains. It was easier to pull heavy loads along the smooth rails than the uneven ground. At first, ordinary flat wheels were used on rails. Then wheels were given edges called "flanges" to help keep them in place.

introduction of a set of gears which he called "sun and planet." Until then, steam engines could produce only an up-and-down movement. The piston made to rise and fall by steam in the cylinder was attached to a beam which also rose and fell. Watt's sun and planet gear enabled the piston to turn a gear wheel, the "planet," which meshed with a second gear, the "sun." The "sun" was connected to a wheel shaft and made it turn.

Watt had found the way to change the up-and-down movement of the piston into a rotary movement. In other words, Watt's sun and planet gears could make steam engines turn wheels. The possibility of steam-powered transport had at last become a reality.

THE FIRST STEAM CARRIAGE

James Watt was not really interested in transport. He designed a steam vehicle in 1784, and his assistant William Murdock (1754–1839) built a working prototype, but the two engineers took the idea no further. It was left to others to explore the possibilities of the steam engine as a means of transport.

In 1770, a Frenchman, Nicolas Cugnot (1725–1804), had made a steam wagon for hauling heavy field guns. Cugnot's wagon had a maximum speed of six miles (ten kilometers) per hour and was not a success. It showed that steam-powered transport was possible, but there was a problem. Efficient steam transport demanded high pressure steam. Could a boiler be made to withstand such high pressure? This difficulty was to hold back many designers of early steam engines.

An English engineer called Richard Trevithick (1771–1833) made a determined effort to solve the problem.

After making a number of successful stationary steam engines for mines, he began to experiment with steam road vehicles. In 1801, he drove his first steam carriage on the road. It had not traveled far before it overheated and exploded, but Trevithick carried on with his work. By 1804, he had succeeded in producing a steam locomotive that hauled a ten-ton load of iron, as well as about seventy people, along a ten mile (sixteen kilometer) length of cast iron railway in Wales.

ON THE RAILS

This was the first time that a steam train had traveled on rails, but the idea of using rails to provide a more even surface than the bumpy, rutted roads of those days was not new. Wooden tramways had been used for horse-drawn transport in coal mines for at least 200 years. About 1800, some of these wooden tracks began to be replaced by longer-lasting cast-iron rails. It was Trevithick's idea of bringing together the iron rails and the steam locomotive that marked the launch of the railway age.

At first, progress was slow. In 1808, Trevithick built a small circular railway track in London to demonstrate his new locomotive, *Catch-Me-Who-Can*. Plenty of people came to see it, but the railway was still seen as a toy, not as a serious means of transport. Trevithick lost heart and turned to other interests.

Meanwhile, steam locomotives had caught the attention of another Englishman, George Stephenson (1781–1848). In 1814, he built his first locomotive for the coal mine where he was the engineer. Eleven years later, his engine *Locomotion* hauled the first railway train on the newly built line, twenty-five miles (forty-two kilometers) long, between Stockton and Darlington in northern England. This was the first railway in the world open to the public, with regular services in each direction. But people were still unsure about the safety of steam travel. Locomotives were used to haul coal trains on the Stockton and Darlington line, but passenger services were horse-drawn.

THE RAINHILL TRIALS

The idea of railways began to catch on, not only in Britain but also in other countries. Plans were made for railway lines in France, the U.S. and Germany. Meanwhile, in Britain, a line was planned between Liverpool and Manchester, a

Cugnot's steam carriage

distance of forty miles (sixty-four kilometers). The directors of the Liverpool and Manchester line were anxious to find the best locomotive for the job, and announced a competition with a prize of £500. It was to be decided by trials over a special length of track at Rainhill, near Liverpool.

The trials were held in October 1829. Ten engineers promised to take part, but in the end only five locomotives turned up for the trials. Two failed to get up enough speed, which left three including *Rocket*, built by George Stephenson and his son Robert (1803–59). *Rocket* was proclaimed the winner when its two rivals suffered burst boilers. Stephenson's prize was not only a check for £500 but also an order for eight similar engines. When the Liverpool to Manchester line opened in 1830, *Rocket* proudly headed the first train.

RAILWAY MADNESS

The success of *Rocket* sparked off a rush to build railways. The first United States line opened in 1830, and soon there was a network of lines linking the important east coast cities with the coal-mining areas of Kentucky and West Virginia. France's first steam railway also opened in 1830 between St. Etienne and Lyons, and Germany followed in 1835. There was such a rush to build railways that people began to speak of "railway madness."

There were rapid improvements in the performance of steam engines, but the railways led to developments in other technologies as well. Building tracks through boggy or mountainous country gave engineers new challenges as they tackled cuttings, embankments, tunnels and viaducts. Many of the lines built then, over 150 years ago, are still used by today's much heavier and faster trains.

ROCKET

SANS PAREIL

PERSEVERANCE

Five locomotives took part in the Rainhill trials. Two of them failed to reach the required speed, Perseverance *and* Cycloped, *a locomotive powered by a horse on a treadmill.* Sans Pareil *and* Novelty *both blew up during the trials, leaving Stephenson's* Rocket *the outright winner.*

NOVELTY

CYCLOPED

Meanwhile, the railways made a vast difference to the lives of ordinary people. Travel was faster and easier than it had ever been. Soon, people were living at a distance from their work and commuting each day by train. The railways made traveling for vacations possible. They also made the transport of goods from place to place easier and cheaper. Fresh meat and vegetables, milk and other dairy products became easier to buy. New towns grew up close to the railway lines. Builders no longer had to depend on local materials, and farmers could transport their cattle to market by train instead of driving them slowly along the roads.

Army generals, too, were quick to realize that railways were an efficient method of transporting troops. The first use of railways in war was in the Crimean War of 1853–56 when Britain and France fought Russia. A temporary railway was built to carry British troops into battle and to evacuate the wounded.

STEAM CONQUERS THE WORLD

Within fifty years of the opening of the first steam-powered railway, the steam locomotive had conquered

RAIL GAUGES

The width of the track between rails is called the gauge. The gauge of the Stockton and Darlington Railway was 56.5 inches (1.435 meters), which was said to be the standard gap between the wheels of wagons used in the area. This gauge was used on most of the railways in Britain and many other parts of the world. But some countries, Russia for example, used a wider gauge. This caused problems when trains were scheduled to cross borders. One solution was to remove the bodies of the carriages by crane and transfer them to wheels of the new gauge. Another answer was adopted in Britain where one railway company, the Great Western, for many years used a gauge of 83.9 inches (2.13 meters). This was to lay an extra rail in between, set to the standard gauge so that trains of either gauge could use the track.

almost the whole world. By 1869, it was possible to cross the United States from the Atlantic to the Pacific by rail. The east-west link across Canada was opened in 1887. India's and Australia's first railways opened in 1854, and Africa's in 1870. Some of these lines gave links with the outside world to places that had been almost completely cut off before.

Most of the world's railways now operate with diesel or electric locomotives, but if it had not been for the pioneers of steam many would not have been built at all.

STEAMSHIPS

Soon after the invention of the steam engine, inventors began to wonder if steam could free sailors from the uncertainties of relying on the wind for power. American engineers led the way in the development of steam for shipping.

Using steam to power ships posed a problem. How exactly was the ship to be pushed forward? James Rumsey (1743–92), an American engineer, built a

△ *Richard Trevithick and his locomotive* Catch-Me-Who-Can.

ship with an engine that pumped water out from the stern. It reached a speed of four miles (six and a half kilometers) an hour in trials on the Potomac River. Another American, John Fitch (1743–98), used oars driven by a steam engine in his ship, the *Experiment*.

Robert Fulton (1765–1815) was more successful. He devised the paddle wheel mounted in the center of the ship. The ship's engine drove a shaft which was the axle of the paddle wheel. As the wheel revolved, its paddles pushed backwards through the water and drove the ship forwards. Fulton's steamship *Clermont* was successful and it began making regular passenger trips in 1807.

△ *A Mississippi sternwheeler.*

STEAM AT SEA

At first, steamships were used only on rivers and canals or for short voyages within sight of land. For work on the Mississippi River in the United States, shipbuilders developed a design with a large paddle wheel at the stern. These ships were called "sternwheelers." Only the lower part of the paddle wheel went under water, so that sternwheelers could be used where the water was shallow.

Taking a steamship out into the ocean was a bigger challenge. No one knew how a ship with a heavy engine would behave in rough seas. The huge amount of fuel used by early engines was another problem. But in 1819, an American ship, the *Savannah*, became the first steamship to cross the Atlantic. Like all the early

oceangoing steamers, the *Savannah* also had sails for use if the engine broke down or fuel ran short. In fact, the sails were used for most of the voyage. The first ship to use steam all the way was the Dutch-owned *Curaçao*, which steamed from Rotterdam to the West Indies in 1827. The voyage took a month.

THE GREAT STEAMSHIP RACE

Excitement about crossing the ocean by steam grew. In 1838, there was a race across the Atlantic between two competing British ships, the *Sirius* and the *Great Western*. The Sirius made the voyage from Liverpool to New York in eighteen days, but towards the end the cabin furniture and even one of the masts had to be used as fuel. The *Great Western* took only fifteen days, and arrived with plenty of coal to spare.

It was a British shipowner, Samuel Cunard (1787–1865), who started the

first regular steamship service across the Atlantic, carrying mail, in 1840. The company he started is still operating ships today. Soon, regular services carrying passengers, mail and cargo were crisscrossing the world's oceans. But the days of the paddle steamer were soon to come to an end.

In 1839, an Englishman, Francis Smith (1808–74), and a Swede, John Ericsson (1803–89), both built ships with screw propellers instead of paddles. They were found to go faster and use less fuel. American shipbuilders were slow to use propellers, but several European shipping companies were soon building new propeller ships for the North Atlantic crossing. In the end, the propeller won, and as the old paddle steamers wore out, they were replaced by propeller ships.

STEAM SHRINKS THE WORLD

Just as railways opened the way to the interiors of the continents, so steamships

brought the continents closer together. Farmers and manufacturers found new markets for their products overseas, carried quickly and reliably by steamer. The steamship was also responsible for large movements of populations, as millions of people from Europe crossed the oceans to begin new lives in North America, Australia and New Zealand.

Within less than a hundred years, steam had changed the world. In 1800, the fastest means of transport on land had

△ *Steam provided oceangoing ships with a reliable source of power and speed that they had never known before.*

been on horseback. At sea, travelers had depended on the way the wind blew. By 1900, there were few large towns or cities in the world without a railway station, and travel by rail had become fast and cheap. At sea, a network of regular steamship services carried passengers and cargoes across the world.

INTERNAL COMBUSTION

The twentieth century has been the age of internal combustion. Today, millions of cars powered by internal combustion are used for getting to work, going shopping, or taking vacations, and making cars is one of the world's major industries.

T here is an important difference between a steam engine and an internal combustion engine of the kind used in cars and trucks. In a steam engine, the fuel is burned in a separate boiler to make steam, which in turn provides the force to make the engine work. In an internal combustion engine, the fuel is burned inside the engine itself. This makes the internal combustion engine a lighter, more compact and more easily controllable machine than the steam engine.

THE GUNPOWDER ENGINE
The story of the internal combustion engine begins over 300 years ago with a Dutch scientist called Christian Huygens (1629–95). About 1680, he built an engine which used gunpowder as fuel. The

△ *The earliest powered vehicles used steam to drive them. Steam carriages never became popular because they were not efficient.*

▷ *Many people were terrified by the first cars. The noisy, smelly vehicles also caused accidents by frightening horses. Until 1896 in England, there was a law that a man had to walk ahead of each car carrying a red flag in warning.*

explosion of the gunpowder raised a piston inside a cylinder, which fell again as the hot gases from the explosion cooled. Today, it sounds rather strange and highly dangerous to run an engine on gunpowder, but Huygens had the right idea. All internal combustion engines are driven by explosions. A modern car engine works because of the explosions of a mixture of fuel and air which take place all the time the engine is running.

The idea of internal combustion was forgotten in the excitement over steam, and it was not until the 1840s that a French inventor, Etienne Lenoir (1822–1900), returned to it. His engine ran on coal gas. It worked well, but it used so much gas that it was not a serious rival to the steam engine.

OTTO'S ENGINE

As with many important inventions, no one person can be described as the inventor of the modern internal combustion engine. Many scientists and inventors tried out different ideas in the middle of the nineteenth century. But in 1878, a German engineer, Nikolaus Otto (1832–91), built the first successful internal combustion engine. His engine was fueled by coal gas, but was not intended for transport. The aim was to find something more compact and convenient than the steam engine to power pumps and factory machines.

The oil industry in those days was very small. Oil was used only for lighting and cooking, and as a lubricant. Some engineers began to experiment with oil as a fuel for engines. Their work developed along two distinct lines and led to the two main types of internal combustion engines that we have today: the diesel engine and the gasoline engine. The gasoline engine was the first to be fitted to a car.

THE COMING OF THE MOTOR CAR

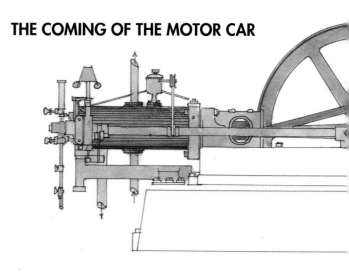

Otto's gas engine, built in 1878, was the first internal combustion engine. It was too heavy to be used in a moving vehicle, but was useful in industry.

Karl Benz

Daimler's gasoline engine was much lighter than Otto's, so it could be used in a moving vehicle.

Gottlieb Daimler

Daimler added an internal combustion engine to a strengthened bicycle to produce one of the first motor vehicles in 1885.

Benz's car still looked rather like a horse carriage used at the time.

BEYOND THE CAR

While some engineers concentrated on using internal combustion to power a "horseless carriage," others saw the possibility of adding it to a bicycle. Bicycles were very popular at the time that the first cars appeared.

The first motorcycles appeared in France and Germany about 1885. They had no gears. The engine drove a leather belt which passed around the hub of the rear wheel. The first two-speed motorcycle was produced in 1902, soon followed by machines with three-speed gearboxes.

Other inventors saw that there was a future for the internal combustion engine for general haulage work and in farming. The first truck to be fitted with an internal combustion engine was built in America in 1902. Soon after, again in America, the first tractor was built for farm use.

One of Otto's assistants was Gottlieb Daimler (1834–1900). Daimler left to set up his own business, and, in the mid-1880s, he began to experiment with gasoline as a fuel. This was mixed with air and drawn into the engine at exactly the right moment when it would explode and drive the piston.

On his third attempt to build his engine, Daimler was satisfied with its performance and fitted it to a bicycle. In 1886, he tried this out on the roads. The next year, he took a four-wheeled carriage, removed the shafts used to attach a horse to it and fitted his engine. This was the first "horseless carriage." In the same year, another German engineer, Karl Benz (1844–1929), fitted a similar engine to a tricycle. He went on to build four-wheeled vehicles.

Daimler's and Benz's cars were the first to go into production for sale to other people. Benz built his own cars, but Daimler sold his engines to a French company, Panhard and Levassor, which built bodies for them. These were the first car bodies that did not copy the design of horse-drawn carriages. The 1894 model had many modern features such as a metal chassis, a hood over the engine, and clutch, brake and accelerator pedals.

The first cars were expensive and were regarded more as toys for rich people than as a serious means of transport. Owners also had to be prepared to have a sense of adventure and an understanding of engines, because breakdowns happened frequently.

As engines became more reliable, more

▽ *Diesel's engine was patented in 1892. It works by igniting oil in compressed air.*

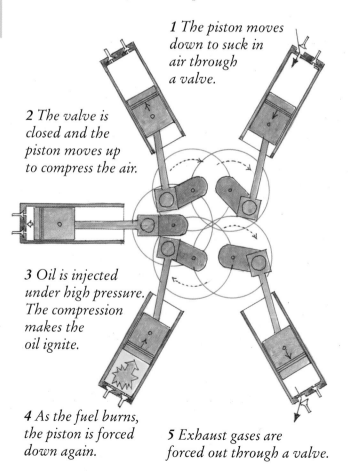

1 The piston moves down to suck in air through a valve.

2 The valve is closed and the piston moves up to compress the air.

3 Oil is injected under high pressure. The compression makes the oil ignite.

4 As the fuel burns, the piston is forced down again.

5 Exhaust gases are forced out through a valve.

people wanted cars, and as more cars were made, the price of them went down. By the 1920s, motoring was beginning to become an everyday experience for millions of people.

THE DIESEL ENGINE

While Daimler and Benz were experimenting with gasoline engines, another German engineer had been working on an internal combustion engine which worked in an entirely different way. Rudolf Diesel (1858–1913) gave his name to the kind of engine fitted to trucks, buses and some cars.

Diesel's engine used an oil similar to paraffin instead of gasoline. It drew air into the cylinder, where it was compressed by the piston. When this compressed air met the fuel which had been forced into the cylinder, the mixture ignited and there was an explosion, forcing the piston upwards.

Diesel patented his engine in 1892, but it was not until 1898 that he demonstrated it at an exhibition in Munich. It was an immediate success despite its size and weight, and was quickly adopted for use in factories. Later, lighter and more compact versions were developed for heavy road vehicles, tractors and eventually for cars.

CHALLENGE FOR THE FUTURE

The internal combustion engine changed the lives of everyone in the twentieth century. We rely on it for personal transport, for deliveries, for emergency services such as fire-fighting and in countless other ways. But it has also brought problems. The most serious of these is air pollution from vehicle exhausts, which has ruined the quality of the air in many cities. The challenge is to develop a means of personal transport which does not damage our health.

THE FOUR-STROKE ENGINE

Otto's engine works on a cycle of four movements.

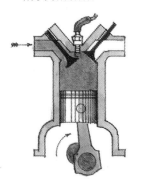

1 The piston moves down and an inlet valve is opened so that gas and air is drawn into the cylinder.

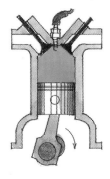

2 The valves are closed and the piston moves back compressing the mixture. A spark ignites the fuel.

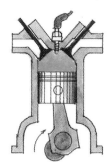

3 The gases in the cylinder expand as they burn, forcing the piston back down.

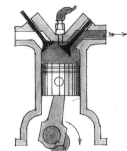

4 Burnt fuel is released through the exhaust valve.

MASS PRODUCTION

*Building a car is a long and complicated job
for one person. But mass production methods
made the job easier and the car cheaper.
It made the dream of owning a car come true
for millions of people.*

There was a time when every article that was made, a clock, a cart, a table or even a gun, was crafted with hand tools and put together by one person in a workshop.

The invention of the steam engine changed all that. Processes such as shaping and polishing wood or metal could now be done by machine much more quickly than by hand. Machines could also make parts which were exactly the same. The processes of manufacture could be broken down into small tasks to make the best use of the workers' skills. So in making a clock, for example, one person could make the gears, another the springs, a third the face and a fourth the case. A fifth person could then put the clock together.

△ *Gun-stock making was one of the first crafts to be taken over by mass production methods, early in the nineteenth century.*

◁ *American Eli Whitney (1765–1825) was a pioneer of mass production, producing guns for the U.S. government. Other arms makers soon adopted the techniques. The most successful was Samuel Colt (1814–62) who produced the famous Colt revolver shown here.*

1 2 3 4 5 6

Today, there is nothing very surprising about this way of working. It is the way most things are made. But 200 years ago, it was something new and strange. The old craft methods had been built up over hundreds of years. Many workers thought that the skills they had painstakingly learned were going to waste. This was partly true. Instead of learning all the different processes of clock-making, for example, a worker could be trained in just one process, such as making the face. But the new method, called "mass production," meant that many articles, from furniture to firearms, became cheap enough for ordinary people to buy.

SPARE PARTS

Mass production was first used in the United States in the manufacture of hand guns at the beginning of the nineteenth century. One advantage appreciated by customers was that if a part developed a

△ Sewing machines were a nineteenth century invention perfectly suited to being mass produced. Large factories, like the Singer factory in the USA, employed thousands of workers.
1 The machine bodies were cast in a foundry.
2 Steam hammers were used to help beat metal parts into shape.
3 Lathes were used to cut screws.
4 Needles, parts which often needed replacing, were manufactured by the thousand.
5 Rows of machines were used for polishing sewing machine parts.
6 The sewing machines were tested before leaving the factory.

fault, it could easily be replaced from a stock of identical parts instead of having to be sent back to the maker for an individual repair. Parts of the same model of revolver could be changed for other identical parts.

Many of the new inventions of the nineteenth century, such as the sewing-machine and the bicycle, were manufactured by mass production methods. But it was the car industry that proved the value of mass production.

The first cars were built by hand in the old-fashioned way. Each part of the engine, for example, was made to fit that particular engine and no other. If it broke or wore out, the manufacturer had to make a new one that would fit exactly, and the owner had to wait while this was done. A small team of workers would build up each car piece by piece. This took a long time and made cars expensive.

The most difficult task in making a car is assembling all its parts. The engine has to be fitted into place on the chassis, followed by the steering-wheel and pedals, the clutch, the gearbox and all the other working parts. Finally, the body of the car has to be built, painted and polished.

CARS FOR EVERYONE

At the beginning of the twentieth century an American carmaker, Eli Ransom Olds (1864–1950), began using some mass production methods. Instead of making all the parts for his Oldsmobile cars in his own factory, he bought in parts made by other manufacturers. These were delivered to the Oldsmobile factory and trundled round on trolleys to the assembly workers.

Another carmaker improved on Olds' methods. Henry Ford (1863–1947) began making cars in 1892. By 1902, he had set up his own business. At that time, motoring was a hobby for the rich. Ford's idea was that if cars could be made cheaply enough, and designed to be reliable, everybody would want one. He was thinking particularly of the farmers of the United States who needed a basic vehicle they could depend on to take them and their families to town and carry farm

BICYCLE POWER

The bicycle became a popular means of transport because it was easily produced by assembling a small number of interchangeable, mass-produced parts. This kept the cost down and made bicycles cheap enough for ordinary people to buy.

The modern bicycle was invented in Britain in 1876, when it was called the "safety bicycle." It quickly replaced the older "penny-farthing" type which had a large front wheel five feet (one and a half meters) in diameter. The first mass-produced safety bicycles were made in 1885 and very soon became popular for travel to work and for leisure cycling.

Part of the success of the bicycle was that, as it was mass-produced, owners could do their own repairs and maintenance by buying spare parts from cycle shops and fitting them themselves.

supplies about their land. The farmers were not rich, and they would have to be persuaded that owning a car was worthwhile. So Ford set about designing a car for them. To keep the price down, he introduced into his factory something which was to revolutionize the manufacture of almost all factory-made products. It was the "assembly line."

On the assembly line, the car's chassis and wheels were put together first. Then they moved on to successive "work stations" where, one by one, the engine,

controls, brakes and other components were added. Finally, complete cars emerged at the end of the line, ready to be tested and sent off to the showrooms. Using this system, Ford cut the time taken to produce a single car from twelve hours to an hour and a half.

THE MODEL T

The car first produced on Ford's assembly line was the Model T, designed with American farmers in mind. It was a huge success and became the most

successful car of all time. The first Model T was built in 1909. By 1925, half the cars in the world were Model Ts, and when production ended in 1927, fifteen million had been made. Model Ts were cheap and reliable. If anything went wrong, spare parts could be found easily at one of the chain of dealers that Ford had set up all across America. The Model T was a triumph for mass production.

Other carmakers were quick to learn a lesson from Henry Ford. Soon, they too put assembly lines into their factories and

△ *Partly finished cars were rolled along the Ford assembly line, and new parts added as they reached various points. Here, the body of the car is being lowered on to the chassis.*

◁ *Henry Ford*

began to compete with Ford's prices and reputation for reliability. By the 1950s, cars were becoming cheap enough for an increasing number of ordinary people to afford. Mass production turned a toy for the rich into an everyday means of transport for almost everyone.

FLIGHT

For centuries, scientists, engineers and amateurs tried to fly with all kinds of strange machines. But it was two bicycle dealers from a small town in the United States who succeeded in making the first powered flight.

T o be able to fly is one of the oldest human ambitions. In the ancient world, people looked at the birds in the sky and envied them. They told stories about imaginary winged gods and goddesses, and about bird-men such as Icarus whose father made him a pair of wings out of wax and feathers. Icarus flew too near the sun, which melted the wax and sent him plunging to his death. In real life, several people tried to imitate Icarus with wings made of various materials, but all with disastrous results.

COPYING THE BIRDS

It was natural that people should think that the way to fly would be to design a machine with flapping wings like a bird's. The famous artist Leonardo da Vinci (1452–1519) made drawings of just such a machine, with wings that were flapped by the pilot's arms, but he never built it.

As it turned out, the first humans to take to the air did so in a very different way. In 1783, two French brothers,

△ *In myth, Icarus flew by attaching bird's feathers to his arms with wax. Early inventors often tried to copy the birds.*

The first human flight was made by the Montgolfiers' balloon in 1783. It was not until the middle of the nineteenth century that powered and steerable airships were produced.

Joseph-Michel (1740–1810) and Jacques-Etienne (1745–99) Montgolfier, built and successfully flew a hot air balloon.

But balloons were at the mercy of the wind for their direction and speed, so they were no use as a means of transport. Attempts to build a true flying machine continued. A number of nineteenth-century experimenters had some success with gliders. An Englishman, Sir George Cayley (1773–1857), designed the first successful passenger-carrying glider in 1853. Cayley worked out the principle of "lift" which is obtained by making the upper surface of the wing convex, and keeps the wing airborne.

The greatest glider pioneer of the age was a German, Otto Lilienthal (1848–96). He made about 2,000 flights in craft he had built himself, but in 1896, a glider that he was flying spun out of control and crashed, killing him. He was only one of many pioneer aviators whose experiments ended in fatal accidents.

FLYING BY STEAM

Other inventors tried making steam-powered aircraft. One of these was Clement Ader (1841–1926), a French engineer. In 1890, he claimed his craft had flown for about 165 feet (fifty meters), but this success was never repeated.

Meanwhile, a number of American inventors had become interested in flying. One, Samuel Langley (1834–1906), built both steam-powered and gasoline-engined aircraft, but neither carried a pilot. The achievement of building the first powered aircraft to make a manned flight went to two American brothers, Orville (1871–1948) and Wilbur (1867–1912) Wright, from Dayton, Ohio.

The Wright brothers ran a bicycle business, but in their spare time they gave all their attention to aeronautics. They had no engineering training, but they studied the scientific principles of flight, read all they could about the pioneer flights of the Europeans and carried out countless experiments with model kites and gliders. They even built their own wind tunnel in their workshop to test the performance of different shapes of wings and propellers.

GETTING IT RIGHT

The Wrights saw that there were three problems to be overcome before powered flight was possible. The first was to make wings large enough to take the weight of the engine and passenger, and to keep the

THE DREAM OF FLIGHT

Before serious experimentation began, many people had wondered about the possibilities of human flight. Many of their ideas look bizarre today, but at the time the experience of flight they had was from watching birds.

Many ancient stories involve people flying relying on magic devices or the power of birds (top left). The first designs for flying machines were often just as impossible, like the airship design (above) which was supposed to be lifted by vacuums in the four spheres. Even the great thinker Leonardo da Vinci failed in his ornithopter design because he forgot to take account of the weight of the wood.

In the nineteenth century, however, inventors such as George Cayley and Otto Lilienthal began to make the dream of flight a possibility.

Leonardo's ornithopter

Leonardo da Vinci

George Cayley

Otto Lilienthal

Lilienthal's glider

Cayley's flying top

Cayley's glider

aircraft in the air. The second was to find the right engine. The third, and perhaps most important, was to work out ways of balancing and steering the aircraft in flight. It was the problem of controlling aircraft in flight that had defeated previous attempts.

The solution that the Wrights worked out to the last problem was to provide their aircraft with controllable surfaces similar to those found on aircraft today. They fitted a movable elevator in front of the wings, and a movable tail fin which acted as a rudder. After experimenting on gliders, in the autumn of 1902, the Wrights set out to build a powered flying machine.

FAILURE AT KITTY HAWK

The Wrights worked carefully, meticulously testing and double-checking each part of their machine as they went along. At last, in December 1903, everything was ready for the great moment. The brothers had chosen for their first flight an area of sandhills called Kill Devil Hills near Kitty Hawk in North Carolina.

Flyer I, as the Wrights named their aircraft, was a biplane with a wingspan of forty feet (twelve meters). It was powered by a four-cylinder gasoline engine mounted in the middle of the lower wing. The engine drove two wooden propellers fitted behind the wings so that they pushed the aircraft through the air. The pilot lay on his front across the lower wing beside the engine, with a bar in front to hold on to. *Flyer I* had no wheeled undercarriage. It would take off from a set of wheels mounted on a rail track, and

Wilbur and Orville Wright

land on skids shaped like skis. Including the pilot, *Flyer I* weighed 750 pounds (340 kilograms).

On December 14, *Flyer I* was placed in position ready for takeoff. Orville and Wilbur tossed a coin to decide who should make the first flight. Wilbur won, and took his position on the lower wing. The engine was started, and *Flyer I*, with Wilbur aboard, began to move along the takeoff track.

Then disaster struck. Perhaps through nerves, Wilbur made a mistake in his setting of the elevator so that *Flyer I* could not rise. It ran to the end of the rail, hit the sand barrier and came to a grinding halt, badly damaged. It must have seemed to the Wrights that all their years of hard work had ended in failure.

TAKEOFF AT LAST

It was three days before repairs to *Flyer I* were finished and the Wrights were ready to try again. This time, it was Orville's turn to be pilot. The engine was started and *Flyer I* began to move. It lifted away from the ground, coming to the ground safely 140 feet (forty-two meters) away.

The first powered flight had lasted a mere twelve seconds, but it was a start. Later the same day, the brothers, taking turns as pilot, made three more flights. On the last of these, Wilbur made up for his mistake of three days before by staying in the air for fifty-nine seconds and covering 750 feet (260 meters) at a top speed of thirty miles (forty-eight kilometers) per hour.

After the fourth landing, the brothers left *Flyer I* standing on the sand and took a much-needed break. While they were

△ The Wright brothers tested and re-tested everything before they attempted powered flight. Soon they were taking longer and longer flights, learning to control the aircraft in the air.

DOGFIGHTS

Early in World War I, aircraft were used for the first time to observe and report on enemy movements at the battlefront. These were small single or two-seater fighters armed with machine guns. Later in the war, heavier aircraft carried out bombing missions over enemy territory.

There was bitter rivalry between the fighter pilots of the warring countries. The "dogfights" between them provided an exciting show for people on the ground, but the fights often ended in the death of one or both pilots.

The most famous of the World War I fighter pilots was a German, Baron Manfred von Richtofen (1892–1918). He was nicknamed "the Red Baron." He claimed to have shot down eighty enemy aircraft in dogfights. He died just before the war ended, shot down behind British lines.

standing talking, the wind got up, and a sudden gust caught the plane. The wings lifted, and the light aircraft rolled helplessly over and over. When it stopped, its wings were damaged, some of their supports were smashed and the engine had broken adrift. On its day of glory, the Wrights' first aircraft had made its last landing. For the brothers, it was back to the drawing board to start designing *Flyer II*.

CRASHING SILENCE

You might think that the Wrights' four successful flights would have made headline news all over the world the following morning. But amazingly, the story didn't even make the pages of the local morning paper in the Wrights'

hometown. People who went in for flying were often written off as cranks attempting the impossible. Even if it were possible, others said, it would be done by trained engineers, not by a couple of small-town enthusiasts. So the Wrights' achievement went almost unnoticed. This did not worry them much. They were convinced, whatever anyone else thought, that powered flight had a future. The brothers returned to their workshop and started planning the improvements they were going to make in *Flyer II*.

The Wright brothers knew that there was a long way to go before flying would be completely safe and reliable. With *Flyer II* and *Flyer III* , they gradually increased the length of their flights and the maneuverability of their aircraft in the air. In October 1905, *Flyer III* flew for a total of thirty-eight minutes, covering twenty-four miles (thirty-eight kilometers). The flight included demonstrations of banking, turning, circling and flying a figure of eight.

SELLING THE IDEA

By now, the Wright brothers were convinced that aircraft had a useful future and planned to go into business making them. But who would buy one? They tried the United States Army, suggesting that aircraft could watch enemy positions from the air and carry messages. At first, the Army was not interested, so in 1908 Wilbur set off for Europe by ship with a demonstration machine.

Europe welcomed flying with enthusiasm. The kings of the United Kingdom, Italy and Spain came to see Wilbur Wright's demonstration. More importantly for the future of flying, so did Lord Northcliffe (1865–1922), the owner of a British newspaper, the *Daily*

Mail. The *Mail* splashed the news of a prize for the first person to fly across the English Channel from France to England. This spurred on both amateur and professional engineers to have a go at making their own machines. The prize was won in 1909 by a Frenchman, Louis Blériot (1872–1936). By this time, everyone was talking about flying. At last, people began to see what it could mean. The Wrights had all the publicity they needed. The air age had arrived.

AIRCRAFT AT WAR

It was not long before the reason for Europe's keen interest in aircraft became clear. Rivalry between Britain and Germany for industrial power, and the old enmity between Germany and France, were leading steadily towards war. When war came in 1914, aircraft were to play a small but important part in it. By now, aircraft could reach speeds approaching 100 miles (161 kilometers) per hour. Germany, France, Britain and

▷ *After World War I, flying circuses became a popular attraction. People would gather to see the flimsy flying machines loop-the-loop and fly upside down. Some people had their first taste of flying at these events, paying to go up for short flights.*

Italy all produced small fighter aircraft like the British Sopwith Camel for use at the fighting front, and heavier bombers to make raids deep into enemy territory. The need for better weapons was a spur to improvements. Most governments added a third fighting service, an air force, to the old forces of the army and navy.

FLYING FOR PEACE

In 1919, the airfields of Europe and America were full of aircraft, and there were thousands of trained pilots and navigators. But could flying could be adapted for peaceful uses?

Charles Lindbergh

transatlantic solo flight from east to west. The first flight across the Pacific was by two Australians, Charles Kingsford Smith (1897–1935) and Charles Ulm (1898–1934), in 1928.

Women too took part in these pioneer flights. Amy Johnson (1903–41), an Englishwoman, flew solo from Britain to Australia in 1930, and followed this up with many other record-breaking flights. The American Amelia Earhart (1898–1937) became the first woman to fly the Atlantic in 1932. Five years later, Earhart

The years after World War I were a time when aviators competed with each other to score "firsts." In 1919, two British fliers, John Alcock (1892–1919) and Arthur Whitten Brown (1886–1948), made the first flight across the Atlantic.

In 1927, an American, Charles Lindbergh (1902–74), made the first solo transatlantic flight from New York to Paris. Five years later a Scottish pilot, James Mollison (1905–59), made the first

disappeared in an attempt to fly around the world from California.

POST IN THE AIR

By this time, flying was not just a matter of a few enthusiasts making record-breaking flights. Governments and business people alike had begun to recognize it as a useful and profitable means of transport. The postal services were among the leaders in taking advantage of the speed of flying.

The very first airmail service began as early as 1911 in Britain. Letters and postcards were carried between London and Windsor as part of the celebrations for the coronation of King George V, but the service operated for only a few weeks.

In 1919, the British Post Office started a regular airmail service between London and Paris. This was later extended to other European cities and by 1921 to the Middle East. Meanwhile, in 1920, the United States Post Office began flying mail between San Francisco and New York, with a number of stops on the way.

THE FIRST AIRLINES

By the 1920s, most people were used to seeing aircraft in the air, and flying no longer seemed to be defying nature. Flying was still considered a sport or a novelty, and many people had their first experience of flying when they went up for "joy rides" lasting for a few minutes. But would they travel by air?

A number of airlines were founded in the 1920s, particularly in countries like Britain, France and the Netherlands which had large empires scattered across the world. The first passenger planes were tiny, some carrying only eight passengers. Some early airlines flew wartime bombers which had been fitted with seats, and some seated their passengers in loose wicker armchairs. But soon the aircraft industry began to build planes specially designed for comfortable passenger travel.

THE DAKOTA

In the USA, where there were huge overland distances to be covered, air travel really took off. American aircraft builders moved into the lead, and 1936 saw the first flight of a plane that was to

ALCOCK AND BROWN

John Alcock and Arthur Whitten Brown made the first nonstop flight across the Atlantic in 1919. Twenty-seven-year-old Alcock was a test pilot for the Vickers Aircraft Company. He chose a World War I Vickers Vimy two-engined bomber, fitted with extra gasoline tanks, for the flight. Brown, who was thirty-three, went with him as navigator.

On June 14, 1919, the two men set out from St John's, Newfoundland in Canada. Sixteen hours and twelve minutes later they landed at Clifden, County Galway in Ireland.

Alcock and Brown shared a prize of £10,000 given by the British newspaper the *Daily Mail*. Both were also given knighthoods. But for Alcock, the triumph was short-lived. Six months later, he crashed and was killed while flying from England to France.

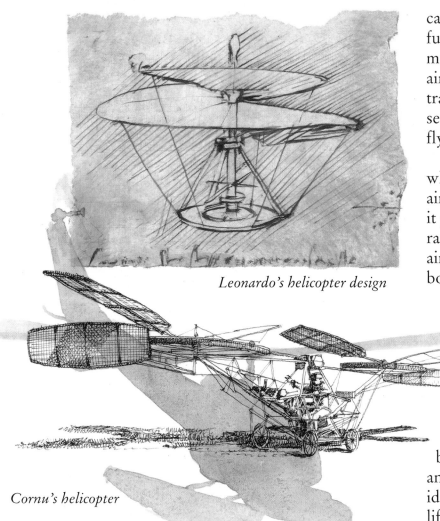

Leonardo's helicopter design

Cornu's helicopter

carry larger amounts of fuel. They soon took over many of the world's longer air routes. The first transatlantic passenger services were operated by flying boats in 1938.

It was only after 1945, when improvements in aircraft technology made it possible to build long-range conventional aircraft, that the flying boat went out of favor.

THE HELICOPTER

Meanwhile, an entirely different kind of aircraft, the helicopter, had appeared. Helicopters use spinning rotor blades to move forward and also to hover. The idea of giving an aircraft lift by spinning some kind of device above it was an old one. In the early sixteenth century, Leonardo da Vinci drew a sketch of such a machine, with a platform suspended from large spinning blades.

Sir George Cayley, the British inventor who had experimented with gliders, began to work on the idea of the helicopter some 300 years after Leonardo. In 1843, he produced a steam-powered design, but it was never built. A real helicopter had to await the invention of the internal combustion engine.

dominate air travel for many years. This was the Douglas DC3, or Dakota. It carried twenty-one passengers and flew at about 165 miles (270 kilometers) per hour. The DC3 became the most widely used plane among the world's airlines, carrying mail, passengers and cargo over short distances. By 1944, over 10,000 were flying. Some are still in use today.

FLYING BOATS

Problems began to emerge as more heavily laden airliners took to the skies. They needed increasingly long runways and also had to make frequent stopovers to take on more fuel. In the 1930s, a new kind of airliner appeared. Flying boats took off and landed on water, and could

GROUND TEST

The attraction of an aircraft which could take off and land vertically, avoiding the need for runways, continued to appeal to engineers, and in 1917 the first working helicopter was made by Louis-Charles Breguet (1880–1955). Four large rotors, or sets of circulating blades, were arranged around the pilot, who sat in the center of the machine. The helicopter never actually took off. It was tested while tethered to the ground, but it achieved a lift of five feet (150 centimeters).

In the same year, another Frenchman, Paul Cornu (1881–1944), made a helicopter which actually made a few brief, low flights. But he had to abandon his experiments because of lack of money.

THE AUTOGIRO

The next important step came in 1923 in Spain, when Juan de la Cierva (1895–1936) demonstrated an aircraft which he called an "autogiro." This had a four-bladed rotor above the fuselage, but each blade was hinged so that it could move up and down during flight. Unlike

▽ *The hovering ability of the helicopter makes it a vital tool for rescue services. It can hover over a spot that is inaccessible otherwise, so that rescue workers can be lowered in and injured people can be carried away.*

a helicopter, the autogiro's rotor blades were not driven by the engine. They went around as the aircraft was driven forward by its propeller. In fact, the autogiro was part helicopter and part airplane. It could not take off or land absolutely vertically, but it did so at a steep angle, avoiding the need for a large airfield. Unlike a helicopter, it could not hover.

Many enthusiasts thought the autogiro might develop into an aerial form of personal transport. Nothing came of these hopes, because the autogiro was overtaken by the helicopter, which could take off and land vertically.

The inventor of the first successful helicopter was Igor Sikorsky (1889–1972). He had experimented with helicopters in Russia, his home country, since 1909, but then turned his interest to fixed-wing aircraft. In the 1930s, he came back to helicopters, and in 1939, his first successful machine, the VS-300, made its maiden flight. Since then, the helicopter has found many uses, like personal transport, troop-carrying, search and rescue work, and in industry.

THE
JET ENGINE

*On the eve of World War II, unknown to each other,
a German and a British inventor
raced against time to produce a jet-engined
aircraft. Their work resulted in the fast, comfortable
intercontinental air travel we enjoy today.*

A lthough jet aircraft were not flown regularly until the 1940s, the idea of an engine producing power by shooting out a stream of gases and compressed air behind it goes back a long way. It is said that the British scientist Sir Isaac Newton (1642–1727) thought of using the idea in a steam carriage as long ago as 1687. Two hundred years later an airplane driven by steam jets was designed, although it was never built.

Then, at the beginning of the twentieth century, the gas turbine was invented.

This works by using hot exhaust gases to drive a turbine, in a similar way to a jet engine. Gas turbines were used in industry, and some people began to wonder if they could be adapted to power aircraft.

THE FIRST JET ENGINE

One such person was a British Royal Air Force officer, Frank Whittle (1907–). Whittle began researching the idea of a gas turbine aircraft engine while he was still a student. By the time he was

△ *The Messerschmidt 262 fighter jet.*

76

THE GAS TURBINE
In a gas turbine, exhaust gases from burning fuel and air
are directed on to the turbine blades.
This provides power to drive the shaft of a machine.

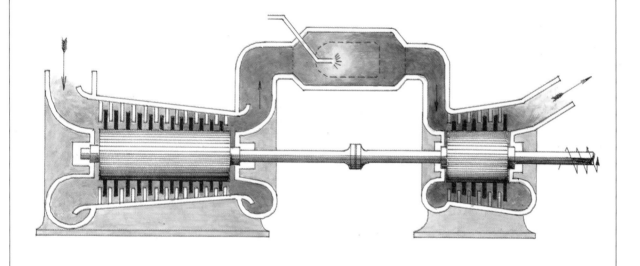

twenty-three, he had designed a jet engine for use in aircraft, although he lacked the money to build one himself. His RAF employers allowed him time off to work on the project, but showed little interest in the results.

Finally, in 1937, Whittle found some backers to finance the building of his jet engine. This was given its first test runs in the same year. There were initial troubles, but Whittle and his team carried on. Then, in 1938, with war looming, the RAF began to take an interest in Whittle's work and gave him the support he needed to speed it up. Two years later, the engine was ready to go into production, and Britain's top engineering firm, Rolls-Royce, was chosen to make it.

Frank Whittle

RACE WITH THE GERMANS
Meanwhile, unknown to Whittle, a German aeronautical engineer was working on similar lines. His name was Hans Pabst von Ohain (1911–).

Unlike Whittle, von Ohain did not have to struggle to find backers. One of Germany's leading manufacturers of aircraft, Heinkel, gave him a job and all the research support he needed. Von Ohain was later than Whittle in producing his first engine, but he was the first to get a jet-engined aircraft into the air, on August 27, 1939, just one week before World War II broke out. It was May 1941 before the first British jet aircraft, the Gloster Whittle E28, was ready to fly.

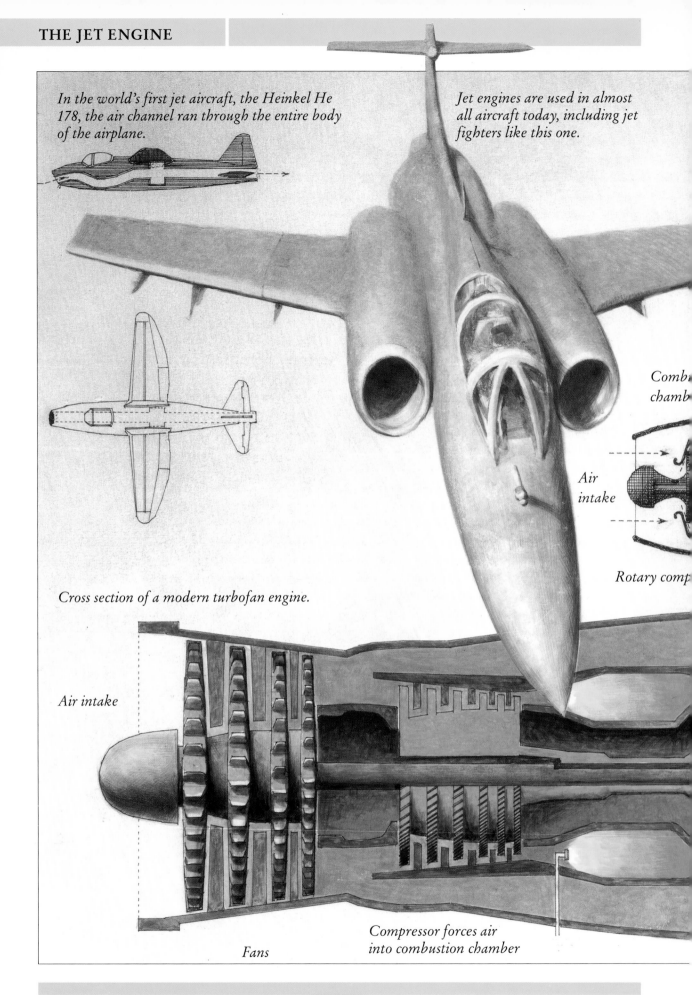

In the world's first jet aircraft, the Heinkel He 178, the air channel ran through the entire body of the airplane.

Jet engines are used in almost all aircraft today, including jet fighters like this one.

Comb
chamb

Air
intake

Rotary comp

Cross section of a modern turbofan engine.

Air intake

Fans

Compressor forces air
into combustion chamber

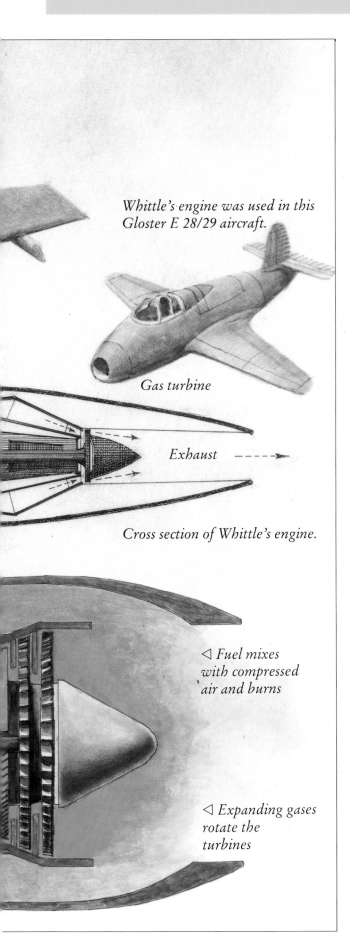

Whittle's engine was used in this Gloster E 28/29 aircraft.

Gas turbine

Exhaust - - - - →

Cross section of Whittle's engine.

◁ Fuel mixes with compressed air and burns

◁ Expanding gases rotate the turbines

JETS AT WAR

Events move quickly in wartime, and both the British and German air forces hurried to build jet aircraft. Their first jet fighters went into service in 1944, just as World War II was reaching its crucial final stages. The increased speed of jet aircraft enabled them to move swiftly into action, surprising the crews of slower piston-engined planes.

The first aircraft to go into production using Whittle's jet engine was the twin-engined Gloster Meteor which could reach a speed of 390 miles (625 kilometers) per hour. The first German jet fighter was the Messerschmidt 262, also twin-engined. The 262 could out-fly the Meteor with a maximum speed of 540 miles (869 kilometers) per hour, but because it had been rushed into service too soon, it had some troublesome design faults. In spite of a few problems in the remaining years of World War II, both of these aircraft demonstrated that the jet engine provided air forces with a powerful new weapon.

Meanwhile, in the U.S., a team of Whittle's engineers had been advising the United States Army Air Force on jet engines. The first American jet, the Lockheed Shooting Star, first flew in October 1942, but the war had ended before it went into service with the U.S. Air Force. Soon, Russia had its first jet aircraft, the MiG 15, and other countries followed suit.

JET AIRLINERS

When peace came in 1945, the jet technology that had been developed for use in warplanes could be applied to civilian aircraft. One of the problems for airlines before the war had been the inefficiency of piston engines. This meant that they had to carry huge amounts of fuel, and even then had to make frequent stops to take on more. The greater efficiency of jets made the development of jet airliners attractive, especially for intercontinental flights. Not only could jets fly faster, they could also fly higher. This improved their efficiency even more, and also gave a smoother and more comfortable flight for passengers as jets could fly above the clouds, so avoiding any bad weather.

As the new jet airliners carrying larger numbers of passengers came into service, the cost of air travel fell. In the United States, even in the 1930s, it had become commonplace to make long journeys between the major cities by air. Now, all over the world, flying lost its pre-war luxury image and became the normal means of travel for people going abroad on vacations or business trips. A new generation of airliners, the huge jumbo jets, was built to cope with the vast numbers of people who now wanted to travel by air.

A whole family of jet engines had been developed from the simple original design. One of these was the turbofan. The front cover of the engine conceals a fan which sucks air in and passes it to a compressor before the air and fuel mixture is ignited. The turbofan operates more quietly and uses less fuel than other types of jet engine. Turbofans were used to power the new wide-bodied jumbos.

FASTER THAN SOUND

Once the jet engine had been developed, the race was on to build engines that would drive aircraft at ever greater speeds. The lead was taken by the world's major air forces. They wanted jet fighters that could fly faster than the enemy's, and jet bombers that could fly high and fast, out of reach of enemy defenses.

"Breaking the sound barrier" became an important target. Sound travels in air at about 720 miles (1,160 kilometers) per hour. At one time, it was thought that at speeds like this the pressure on aircraft frames, and on the bodies of their pilots,

▽ Concorde *has a cruising speed of 1,425 miles (2,300 kilometers) per hour.*

JUMP-JETS

The thrust of gases from a jet engine pushes an aircraft forwards. Some engineers reasoned that if this thrust was pointed towards the ground, it would also give an aircraft enough lift to take off. This reasoning has led to the development of vertical takeoff and landing aircraft, or "VTOLs," for military use. Warplanes are often required to take off from ships or in other confined spaces. VTOLs can operate from clearings. VTOLs are among the fastest small aircraft carriers or from jungle and most agile aircraft in the sky today.

would be too much. This was disproved in 1947 when an American Bell X-1 aircraft, powered by a rocket engine, broke the sound barrier without mishap. There was no reason why suitably designed aircraft should not fly at supersonic speeds.

SUPERSONIC PASSENGER TRAVEL

Once this was known, the world's air forces began to equip themselves with supersonic bombers and fighter aircraft. Airlines, too, were attracted by the thought of supersonic flight. The costs of developing a supersonic airliner are huge, and so far only two have ever gone into service. One was the Russian Tupolev 144, and the other was *Concorde*, jointly developed by Britain and France.

Concorde began regular flights across the Atlantic in 1976.

Both planes were disappointments. The Tupolev 144 had technical problems and was withdrawn from regular use. *Concorde* has never earned the money that was spent on it. This is partly because it carries only 128 passengers, making fares very expensive. There are other problems with *Concorde*, too. It is also extremely noisy and needs a very long runway for takeoff and landing.

Although *Concorde* can cross the Atlantic twice as fast as a conventional jet, most people prefer to continue to travel slower but more cheaply. Scientists are still working on jet technology, to try to achieve supersonic speed at a lower cost and with less noise.

ROCKETS

When the ancient Chinese let off the first rockets, they could not have dreamed that these toys would one day lead to the exploration of space, landings on the moon and worldwide communications.

L ike a jet engine, a space rocket uses the backward rush of exhaust gases to propel itself forward. In a jet engine, the gases are produced by the burning of fuel mixed with the oxygen found in the Earth's atmosphere. But a space rocket contains its own supply of oxygen as well as the fuel to be burned with it. This is why space rockets are able to continue to operate outside the Earth's atmosphere, for as long as their fuel lasts. But the very first rockets had nothing to do with space travel at all.

THE FIRST ROCKETS

The ancient Chinese were probably the first people to use rockets made with gunpowder as fireworks. They probably also attached rockets to arrows. Although not very accurate, these missiles would certainly have frightened the enemy.

△ *In ancient China, rockets were used as fireworks or as weapons to terrify enemies.*

▷ *The unknown realms of space have been the subject of many books and films. Space travel was a fantasy when Jules Verne and H.G. Wells wrote about it, but today it is reality. How many other space fantasies will become facts in the future?*

△ *In the eighteenth century, Indian prince Hyder Ali built explosive rockets as weapons.*

Knowledge of gunpowder passed from China to Europe by way of the Islamic world. About 1250, the English scientist Roger Bacon (c. 1214–1292) wrote down the formula for gunpowder. About a hundred years later a German monk, Berthold Schwarz (fourteenth century), invented the first firearms. Soon gunpowder was being produced all over Europe for use in guns, and inventors began to think about using it in rockets.

ROCKETS AT WAR

One of the most successful such inventor was an eighteenth century Indian prince, Hyder Ali (1728–82). He and his son Tippu Sultan (1749–99) built rockets with a metal container in which the fuel was burned. The metal containers could withstand greater explosions, giving the rockets more thrust. These Indian rockets were used in battles against the British in India in 1792 and again in 1799.

The British were impressed and began to investigate rockets for themselves. Sir William Congreve (1772–1828), a scientist employed by the British army, worked on the idea. By 1805, he had developed a rocket for use at sea as an attack weapon. It was first used in the following year, both at sea and on land. Congreve's rocket was so successful that a Rocket Brigade of the British army was formed to specialize in rocket warfare. But improvements in firearms and artillery made them more accurate and efficient than rockets, so the science of rocket warfare was abandoned for a time.

DREAMS THAT CAME TRUE

The idea of traveling into space with the help of rockets was first put forward by writers of science fiction. In 1865, the French writer Jules Verne (1828–1905) published a story called *From the Earth to the Moon*. The British author H. G. Wells (1866–1946) also wrote about adventures in space involving rocket propulsion. Although these stories were fiction, they were based on real scientific theories. It is surprising how close to the reality of space travel many of their ideas were.

▷ *Although Verne's and Wells' stories were works of the imagination, they were based on scientific theories of the time. The first space rockets reflected their stories and the first moves towards rocket-powered travel began only fifty years after Verne published* From the Earth to the Moon.

1 *Tsiolkovski's space ship*
2 *Goddard's liquid-propelled rocket*
3 *German V-2 rocket*
4 *Modern multistage rocket*
5 *Multistage rocket showing its different stages*
6 *The* Saturn V *rocket, which took the manned* Apollo *craft to the moon.*

1

2

3

4

5

6

LIQUID FUEL

In Russia, Konstantin Tsiolkovski (1857–1935) began to write seriously about the possibilities of space travel in 1895. He had given some thought to the problem of making a rocket powerful enough to escape from the Earth's gravitational pull. Tsiolkovski's idea was to use a mixture of liquid hydrogen and oxygen as fuel.

At about the same time, in the United States, an American teenager called Robert Goddard (1882–1945) was thinking about the possibility of traveling to Mars. It was believed in the 1890s that the so-called canals observed on Mars by astronomers were evidence that some form of human life existed there. So Mars became the focus of scientists' thoughts about space travel.

Robert Goddard became fascinated with thoughts of rocket-powered travel in space. He became a leading physicist and a professor at Clark University in Massachusetts. In 1914, he began designing rocket engines, and five years later published a forecast that rockets would one day carry a camera to the dark side of the Moon.

Yuri Gagarin, the first man in space.

By 1926, Goddard was ready to test his first liquid-propelled rocket. In 1930, one of his rockets reached a height of 2,000 feet (610 meters), travelling at 500 miles (804 kilometers) per hour. Five years later, he sent up a rocket which broke the sound barrier.

ROCKETS AT WAR

Robert Goddard's work was reported in scientific journals and aroused interest in Europe. Societies for rocket research and space exploration were formed. One of these was based in Berlin, Germany, and was founded by a young engineering student, Wernher von Braun (1912–77). His society obtained the use of a plot of land near Berlin as a rocket-launching site. By 1931, one of von Braun's rockets had reached a height of one mile (1.609 kilometers).

At this time, the German government was forbidden to make weapons by the Peace Treaty after World War I. But the Treaty said nothing about rockets, so the government funded von Braun's rocket research. He turned his attention from space travel to weaponry, and in 1936, he was put in charge of a secret rocket research station at Peenemünde. It was here that he developed the *V-2* guided missile, a terrifying weapon launched against Britain in the closing stages of World War II. By April 1945, 4,000 *V-2*s had been fired.

RIVALS FOR ROCKETRY

It was clear that Germany was the world leader in rocket technology and that rockets provided a means of delivering powerful weapons over long distances. The two rival superpowers, the U.S. and the then U.S.S.R., both wanted German rocket technology. Wernher von Braun, who had surrendered to the American army in 1945, went with his team to the United States. Other German scientists went to the U.S.S.R. The division of knowledge about rockets led to the "space race" of the 1960s and 1970s between the superpowers. At the same time, both

SPACE LITTER

In the past thirty years, hundreds of satellites have been launched into orbit. Some were programmed to send back information for a limited period of time, and then stop. Others never functioned properly, and simply keep on going round uselessly. There is no way of knowing how many pieces of this space junk are still in orbit around the Earth, or even further out in space beyond orbit. Some are diverted off course by collision with meteorites and veer towards the Earth, burning up as they reach the atmosphere. The rest, out of control because their communications systems are broken, may continue to orbit the Earth for centuries.

There are also tools and pieces of equipment which have been lost or dumped by astronauts. Lunar vehicles have been abandoned on the moon, and some of the planets now carry the remains of space probes which have been deliberately crashed into them. The people of the Earth have explored space but they have also polluted it.

▽ *Neil Armstrong, Buzz Aldrin and Michael Collins who traveled to the moon in Apollo 11.*

competed to develop rocketry as a method of delivering nuclear weapons.

RUSSIA SCORES A FIRST

Both the U.S. and the U.S.S.R. worked on similar lines. The first essential in space exploration was to break free of the Earth's gravitational pull. But before that, there was the possibility of putting objects in orbit, held at a distance from the Earth by gravity but still free to circle the planet. In December 1957, the U.S.S.R.'s *Sputnik 1* became the first satellite to achieve this. Its distinctive

"bleep" as it circled the earth became a wonder of the world. The space race was now on in earnest, and America's rocket team, led by Wernher von Braun, redoubled its efforts.

America responded a few months after *Sputnik 1* with its own artificial satellite, *Explorer 1*, but by this time the U.S.S.R. was even further ahead. Just one month after the launch of *Sputnik 1*, they had launched *Sputnik 2*, this time carrying a dog named Laika, the first live passenger in space!

Two years later, the U.S.S.R. was the first to put a manned craft in space, when Yuri Gagarin (1934–68) orbited the Earth. The Americans followed a month later, sending astronaut Alan B. Shepard into space for just fifteen minutes. Then, on July 16, 1969, the world heard that Jules Verne's fantasy of a hundred years before

◁ *As he stepped on to the surface of the moon, Neil Armstrong spoke his famous words, "That's one small step for a man, one giant leap for mankind."*

▽ *The first spacecraft could only be used once, but the space shuttle is designed to be reusable.*

had come true. US astronauts Neil Armstrong (1930–) and Edwin "Buzz" Aldrin (1930–) had landed on the surface of the moon.

A CHANGED WORLD

There have been many exciting space exploits since then, all made possible by rocket technology. But rocket-launched satellites have changed our lives in many more everyday ways. Satellite television has made it possible for us to receive dozens of different programs at home.

News from the other side of the world can be beamed to us by satellite while it is still happening. Satellites carry international telephone calls, keep a watch on the world's weather, provide aids to navigation for sailors and aircrews, report on the movements of troops of potential enemies and provide a wealth of valuable information for astronomers and other scientists. In just a few decades, rocket technology has changed our lives.

FURTHER READING

Atkinson, I. *The Viking Ships*. New York: Cambridge University Press, 1979.

Burnie, David. *Machines and How They Work*. New York: Dorling Kindersley, 1991.

Davies, Eryl. *Transport: On Land, Road & Rail*. New York: Franklin Watts, 1992.

Fisher, Leonard E. *The Ship Builders*. Boston: Godine, 1987.

———. *The Railroads*. New York: Holiday House, 1979.

Ford, Barbara. *The Automobile: Inventions That Changed Our Lives*. New York: Walker & Co., 1987.

Hewish, Mark. *Jets*. London: Usborne, 1991.

Humble, Richard. *Ships: Sailors and the Sea*. New York: Franklin Watts, 1991.

Jefferis, David. *Flight: Fliers and Flying Machines*. New York: Franklin Watts, 1991

Lampton, Christopher. *Rocketry: From Goddard to Space Travel*. Edited by M. Kline. New York: Franklin Watts, 1988.

Macauley, David. *The Way Things Work*. New York: Dorling Kindersley, 1988.

Miller, Marilyn. *The Trans-continental Railroad*. Lexington, MA: Silver, Burdett & Ginn, 1985.

Moolman, Valerie. *The Future World of Transportation*. New York: Franklin Watts, 1984.

Parker, Steve. *The Random House Book of How Things Work*. New York: Random House, 1991.

Platt, Richard. *Stephen Biesty's Incredible Cross-sections*. Illustrated by Stephen Biesty. New York: Knopf, 1992.

Reid, Struan. *Usborne Illustrated Handbook of Invention and Discovery*. London: Usborne, 1986.

Sutton, Richard. *Car*. New York: Dorling Kindersley, 1990.

Taylor, John. *How Cars Are Made*. New York: Facts on File, 1987.

Young, Caroline. *Railways & Trains*. Illustrated by Colin Young. London: Usborne, 1991.

INDEX